CIRCLE BUILDERS

BUILDING SYSTEMS THAT BUILD A COMPLETE LIFE!

STEPHEN MILLER

HIGH BRIDGE BOOKS
HOUSTON

Circle Builders
by Stephen Miller

Copyright © 2023 Stephen Miller

All rights reserved.

Printed in the United States of America
ISBN: 978-1-954943-70-4

All rights reserved. Except in the case of brief quotations embodied in critical articles and reviews, no portion of this book may be reproduced, stored in a retrieval system, or transmitted in any form or by any means—electronic, mechanical, photocopy, recording, scanning, or other—without prior written permission from the author.

Unless otherwise noted, scripture is taken from the New King James Version®. Copyright © 1982 by Thomas Nelson. Used by permission. All rights reserved.

Scripture quotations marked as NASB are taken from the NEW AMERICAN STANDARD BIBLE(r), Copyright (c) 1960, 1962, 1963, 1968, 1971, 1972, 1973, 1975, 1977 by The Lockman Foundation. Used by permission. https://www.lockman.org

High Bridge Books titles may be purchased in bulk for educational, business, fundraising, or sales promotional use. For information, please contact High Bridge Books via www.HighBridgeBooks.com/contact.

Published in Houston, Texas, by High Bridge Books.

CONTENTS

Special Acknowledgment _____v

1. The Circle Consideration _____1
2. The Quest for Spirituality _____21
3. Mastering Your Emotions _____35
4. Grow Your Intellect _____47
5. Fighting for Your Family _____55
6. Intentional Associations _____63
7. Mind Your Temple _____71
8. Improve Your Financial Acumen _____79
9. Your Quality of Life IQ _____89
10. Systems for Circle Building _____95
11. Stellar Work Ethic: _____117

SPECIAL ACKNOWLEDGMENT

SEVERAL YEARS AGO, ON A SATURDAY EVENING at a Starbucks in the Lake Houston area, I sat with my mentor of over 30 years—Dr. Richard Heard. I began to share with him how the idea and teaching of our "measure of rule," or the metron, was igniting my whole philosophy of life and my personal assignment to share it with the world. I laid out all that had evolved within me for the past several years: the premise, graphics, strategic process, and more. It was met with his usual praise accompanied by a further challenge.

He looked at my artwork, notes, and drafts and said, "I think this is powerful and will help people immensely... but you should consider the idea that there are two more core values to add to the five you have identified."

That conversation both expanded and solidified a revelatory ideal that has become my presentation of the "Circle Builders." I hope and pray that understanding and embracing this ideal will do for you what it has done for myself and countless others over the last many years.

Thank you, Dr. Heard, for your friendship and mentorship and for constantly challenging me to dig deeper and go farther.

1

THE CIRCLE CONSIDERATION

JOE AND BRITTANY SAT QUIETLY IN THE EXQUISite lobby of their dream five-star resort hotel. They were in no hurry to leave. It had been such an exceptional and rejuvenating experience. They had both been looking forward to this weekend for a long time and didn't want it to end. With both working full-time jobs, they had needed this getaway badly. They managed to book a three-night stay for their anniversary week. By combining their travel points, a special discount code, and a little bit of help from their kids, they had planned out an amazing retreat together that they would have otherwise never been able to afford. But it had been worth it.

The had even saved some money on the side to splurge on a meal the night before, prepared by their favorite reality-TV show, top-rated Michelin chef. As they sat there looking out the restaurant window, they oohed and awed over one "dream car" after another making their way to the valet—a Bentley, a Porsche, several Rolls Royces, even a couple of Lamborghinis—drive up the circular driveway in luxurious style. They couldn't help but let their minds wonder. Brittany glanced over at Joe—they'd been together long enough for her to know exactly what he was thinking, and she was spot on this time as well—they were both thinking the same thing. They had seen more fit and seemingly happy people in one day than they had in years. They'd watched people toss their black metal Amex cards around freely and knew exactly what that represented.

They'd even overheard several other couples talking at dinner about the scuba trip the week before. Today, a whole group of them were going golfing all day. One of the gentlemen hollered out to another guy, "This was fun, Larry, let's do it again next month." What!? Again? In a month!? They had saved up for months to eke out one dream trip for themselves to remember. They could hardly imagine living this way with any kind of regularity.

Both were moderately pleased with their lives—regular church attendance, a few great friends, a reasonably peaceful family life, and no insurmountable problems. Also, neither of them was completely naive. They knew life wasn't flawless for anyone. And it was safe to assume that these people had at least a few challenges of their own to deal with. Everyone has at least an issue or two as life presents its share of challenges to everybody. But still, they couldn't resist wondering… were they missing something? Were they settling too early? Was there more out there for them?

Neither one of them was overly materialistic either, nor did they have some kind of insatiable appetite for big expensive stuff. It was more of the hugely sought-after quality these visible things seemed to represent. That was it… *freedom*!

Freedom from poverty and scarcity. Freedom from internal chaos and turmoil in their home. Freedom from these nagging health issues. Freedom from the debilitating insecurities and mental hang-ups they dealt with. Freedom from the subtle guilt and shame of feeling like they were never enough, didn't measure up, hadn't accomplished enough, and the list goes on.

What would life be like if money wasn't such a driving concern? What if they had the freedom to live wherever they wanted to live, wear whatever they wanted to wear, and drive whatever they wanted to drive? What if they could both get in shape and be really healthy? How amazing would it be if things were better for them and the kids financially, perhaps elevating their overall quality of life?

What would it feel like to have it all together? What if their relationship with God was healthy enough that they always felt confident, affirmed, and at peace? At the same time, what if they took several vacations a year and had a family that was fulfilled and completely excited about life?

What if they could both, once and for all, eliminate the haunting insecurities and complexes that seemed to paralyze them at times? What would it be like to "have it all?" What if they could destroy that demon called "scarcity" once and for all? So many questions that just wouldn't completely go away.

Joe shook himself slightly—Brittany breathed a sigh... Wow, that would be nice. But just as quickly as their minds had paused long enough to entertain such craziness and briefly escape their "just survive" reality, it snapped right back. Oh well, back to the ole grind.

Back to their jobs they could barely tolerate, the stressful pace they lived, and the exhausting tasks that had become their norm.

I have a few questions for you now. How many times has this been you? How often do you sit and dream about a life that is more? Daydream about what it would be like to *have more, be more, and achieve more*? There's no shame in it. In fact, it may be a good starting point to build the abundant life that God wants for you.

The truth is—not only *can* you have it all, but you *should* have it all! I am aware of how audacious that statement sounds and perhaps conjures up a plethora of emotions and ideas in different people.

The notion of having it all has perhaps been a fleeting component of your imagination or a fantasy, but for most, that's as far as it goes. If you're like a lot of people, you are probably accustomed to brushing those grandiose thoughts out of your mind as quickly as they entered. Totally unrealistic, what a dreamer, and impossible may be just a few of the things you told yourself. But is it really?

What does it even mean to have it all? Is it possible to have it all in this life? Is it realistically attainable? Or are you simply wasting mental energy thinking about a life that could never be?

I must reiterate here from the beginning: I am not promoting the idea that every good person's life should be without challenges, they should all be millionaires, and every day should be like dancing through lily fields without a care in the world.

Perhaps I should start by making a few recommendations concerning the meaning of *all*.

Most people have their own ideas concerning having it all, and most of the time, these ideas are likely to fall woefully short. Or it is an incomplete perspective that involves what I refer to as one- or, at best, two-dimensional success.

The countless people I have interviewed, mentored, or coached, initially described *all* as being something like this:

- To have a body like a Greek god, chiseled and ripped.
- To have enough money to do whatever I want and never have to worry about finances again.
- To get my family together and have peace in my home.
- Or the more spiritually focused one usually says, "I just want to be a really good, moral person."
- To have a relationship with God like never before.

While all of these have merit to them and may be worthy short-term goals, when they are the single, isolated focus, they fall terribly short of giving you that sense of total fulfillment and success. The good life requires more.

The consequences of one- or two-dimensional success are way too often illustrated in people, even driven, talented, and highly capable people. From church leaders, CEOs and executives to the ordinary person, the all-too-familiar observations that I have made usually look something like this:

- The extremely wealthy individual who can't sleep at night because there's no peace.
- The successful and accomplished pro-athlete who can't make a relationship work.

- The young stud of a guy who has a ripped six-pack for abs and a body that looks like Wolverine, but he's a jerk, broke half the time, and can hardly make a relationship work.

- The fantastic husband and father who lives from paycheck to paycheck and can't provide all that he'd like to for his family.

- The financial guru who has no friends or struggles with a debilitating addiction.

- The successful business owner and great family man who is terribly out of shape and will probably die 10–15 years sooner than necessary due to poor fitness and health.

- Or the spiritual godly person whose life doesn't look much different than anyone else's.

The scenarios are endless. Sure, having some success in only one or two values doesn't spell the end of the world for you, but it does indicate a flawed thought process that will keep you in this vicious game of real-life Whack-a-Mole! Solve one issue, and another one pops up. Get momentum in one area, and something else hits a crisis point.

Further, when we don't understand or acknowledge the interconnectedness of all seven values, we also never experience the exponential growth that results from the synergy of simultaneous development of those values. Nor do we realize how the deficiency in one area so adversely affects the others.

THE CIRCLE CONSIDERATION

It doesn't have to be this way. You do not have to choose which area you want to excel in, to the exclusion of others. I want to give you four things to consider in the context of pursuing total life success:

1. I want to help you understand the human experience from a circular perspective rather than a linear one.

2. I want to show you the critical need to value the spiritual, intellectual, emotional, family, social, physical health, and financial as equally achievable and interconnected values in your personal circle.

3. I'm going to show you a proven systematic way to approach growing your personal circle to maximize congruent development in all seven values.

4. Finally, I'm going to show you how to raise your "life quality IQ."

While I will include a plethora of principles as well as references to some of my great friends who are living the "complete life," it will be important to remember that *no one* is always hitting a grand slam in all seven values. And that's okay. That's not how real success is defined anyway. Success is "completeness." And completeness is about equal development and advancement rather than one-value acceleration.

Consider, from the times of early great civilizations, in nearly all of them, their philosophers, spiritual guides, and thought leaders viewed the human experience as one lived *not* from a linear perspective but rather from within a circle. A circle that is comprised of specific dimensions or values. While the specificity of what those values are and how many there are has varied, their similarity and their essentiality have not.

One of the prolific writers of New Testament scripture, the apostle Paul, referred often to this idea of every person having a specific "measure" or sphere of rule in their lives. He refers to a spherical space within from which every one of us lives our lives. It is a space that is specific and exclusive to us that we are gifted and empowered to prosper in.

> For I say, through the grace given to me, to everyone who is among you, not to think of himself more highly than he ought to think, but to think soberly, as God has dealt to each one a measure of faith. (Rom. 12:3)

The ancient Greeks had a particular word as well to describe this spherical personal space. They called it *your metron* (from which the word *matrix* is derived). It simply refers to a spherical shape used to measure. Or the circle in which you do life. And while it is specific to the individual, it is not ambiguous or vague — nor is it subjective.

Centuries of history, experiential reality, extensive research within the psychological community, ancient scriptural wisdom, and good ole common sense have collectively affirmed the certainty of these *seven imperative values of the human experience*.

So, what's the difficulty or great challenge? The challenge is in the way we approach developing and growing our circles. The average person attempts to do so by giving time, energy, and focus to either of two values or constantly waffling in between them… the one that they're best at and is easiest for them and then the one that is in crisis. Not unlike the game of Whack-a-Mole. The inevitable result of trying to follow this method of personal growth and development will always be a one- or two-dimensional life. This is called viewing life from a linear perspective.

The Greeks also used a word to describe what a proper and healthy metron looked like. It is the word *teleios*, which means "the development or completion of growth in all of its parts." Teleios is translated as both "perfect" and "complete."

The revelation is this: systematically and simultaneously developing these seven values, as opposed to addressing one challenge at a time, results in perfection or better understood, "completeness."

This happens because of the exponential growth that comes from the synergy of living systematically as it pertains to your patterns and habits.

And if it is true that life is meant to be lived from within a circle, and your life needs to constantly progress forward and maintain traction, then it becomes imperative to maintain the shape of the circle.

Synergy is a powerful thing. Synergy generally means "the interaction or cooperation of two or more organizations, substances, or other agents to produce a combined effect greater than the sum of their separate effects." The person who can bicep-curl a maximum of 40 pounds with each hand would mistakenly assume that their limit with a barbell and both hands would be 80 pounds. Because of synergy, what they can do with both arms collectively will supersede considerably what they could do with each arm individually.

Likewise, when a person has a system that equally distributes the same amount of time, effort, and attention to the seven values of their life simultaneously, the growth and development will outperform what they could experience through addressing one area or value at a time. And by simultaneous, I am referring to every 24-hour increment of time.

This is vastly critical because of these acts: The inevitable outcome of addressing one value at a time will always produce deficiencies. When you develop and grow one dimension of your life at a time, your circle ceases to be a circle.

So, the perfect or "complete" life is achieved because of simultaneously developing all seven life-values, giving way to an exponential growth in the totality of your life. *This is having it all.*

- Being *spiritually* connected to the divine.
- Being *intellectually* sound.
- Possessing a high *emotional* IQ through self-mastery.
- Building a healthy, happy, and fulfilled *family*/home.
- Having a great *social* circle in which there is mutual benefit and value exchanged.
- Having good *fitness* and living a heavy lifestyle.
- Having good *financial* acumen and financial freedom.

This is the common acceptance of the circle of life matrix. It reflects the seven life-values that are sure to bring you to a place of happiness and fulfillment. It has served as the matrix by which countless people, in their own respective ways, have achieved an unbelievable life in which they can *be* more, *have* more, and *achieve* more… or "have it *all*." This must become your collective system of values if you are going to construct your life for sustainable happiness and success.

You were created and "wired" not only to need development in these seven values but also to thrive because of it. The synergy of equal development given to these core life values causes an exponential growth effect in the totality of your life. I've said for years:

> Success is not measured by the size of your company nor your bank account … rather, success is measured by the congruency in the circumference of your circle.

These values are not a prioritized list of values to be addressed one at a time. They are the core values of true success that must be treated with equal reverence.

Consider your personal circle to be your own "permaculture" (an agricultural system or method that seeks to integrate human activity with natural surroundings to create highly efficient self-sustaining ecosystems).

A few years ago, my middle daughter, Bethanie, spent some time in Mozambique running a project that was based largely on the idea of permaculture. It was this fantastic ranch-type community. They had huge commercial chicken coups. The waste from the chickens was scooped up and thrown on top of the water of the tilapia fish pools—which, when the sun shone through it, created a type of algae for the fish to feed on. When the fish were of an appropriate size, they were traded for corn (some sold for cash). The corn was planted and grew quickly. When they harvested the corn, it was traded in parts—some for consumption, some replanted, some for new chickens, and then some was used to feed the little chickens. And the cycle continued.

When any one of those segments didn't do well or proportionately lagged, it brought a disruption to the whole circle. That's how important it is to manage your personal circle. Creating effective and equal growth in all seven parts so as not to allow disruption in any of them.

Try this exercise to make the reality a bit clearer to you:

Where all the lines intersect in the middle being "zero," and the furthest point outward being "ten," go around the circle and evaluate yourself in terms of development on a scale of 1–10: 1 meaning you have given very little attention to it or perhaps struggle continuously in that area and 10 meaning you're a rockstar who's knocking it out of the park. When you finish all seven values, go clockwise, and connect all the dots. You will end up with a particular shape.

If you erased everything outside of that shape, the question every individual human being should be prepared to answer is…

"WILL MY LIFE ROLL?"

It can look like this:

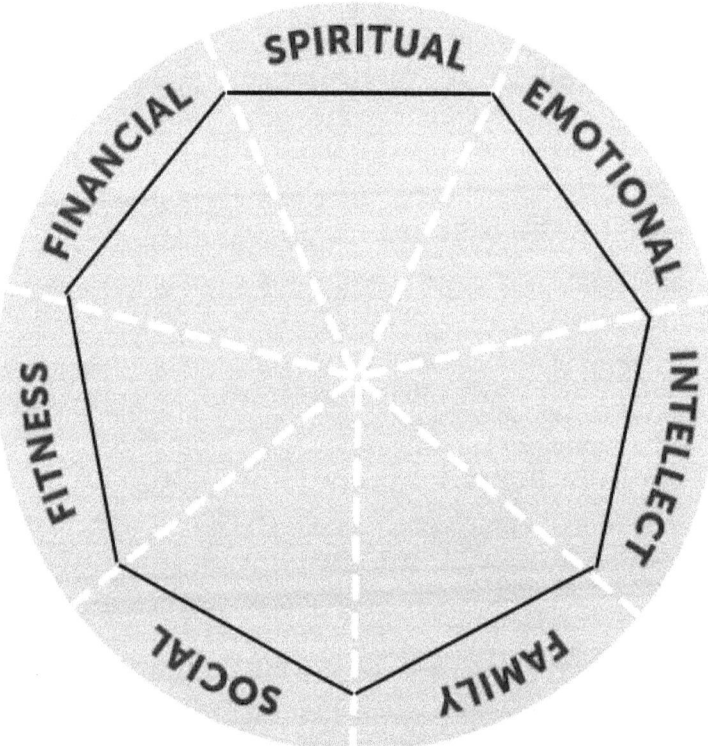

Or even this (barely average in your assessment but developed more completely):

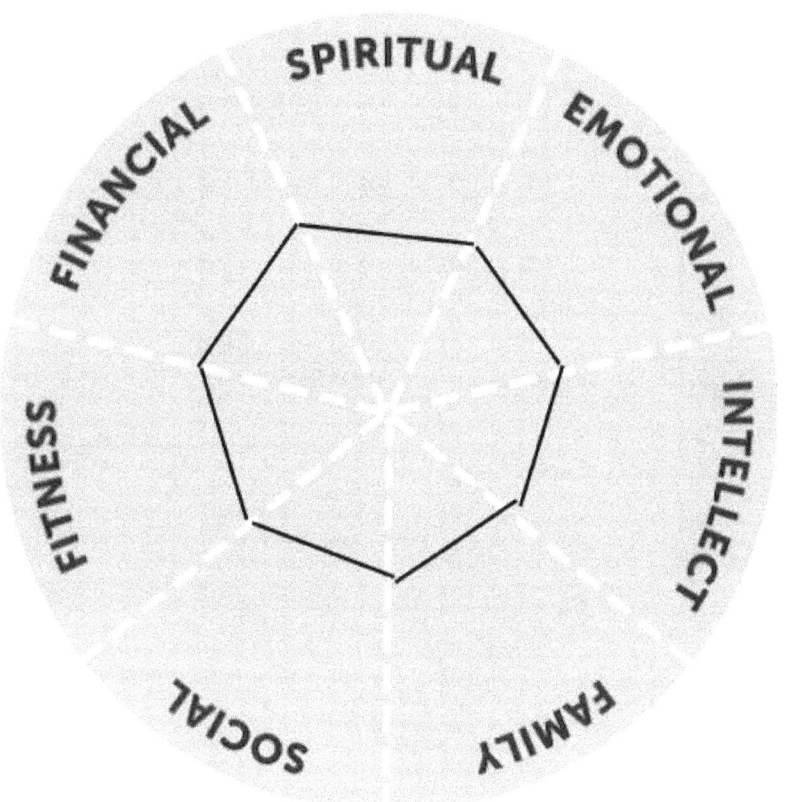

But it cannot look like this:

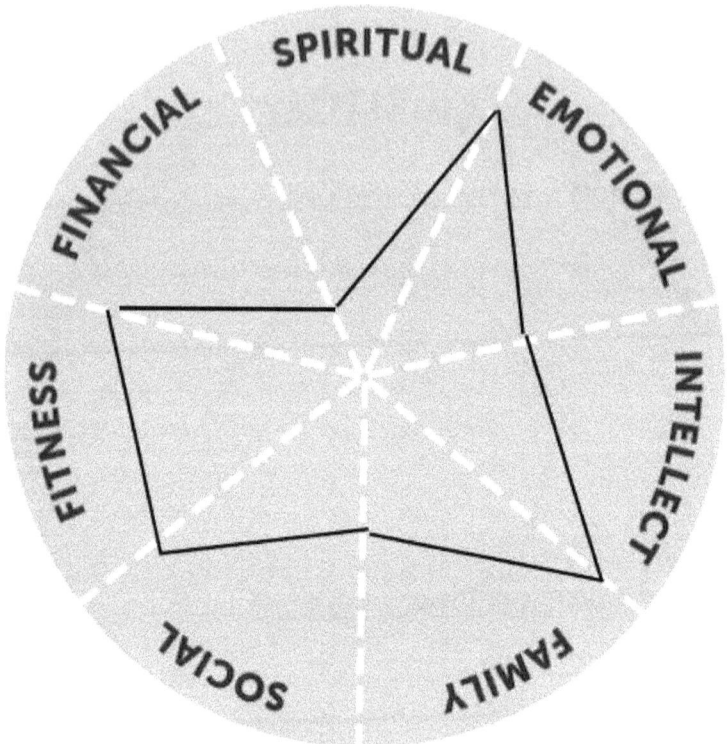

DEFICIENCY BREEDS DEFICIENCY

When it comes to approaching the idea of "all," most people waffle between the value they're more comfortable with or that comes easiest to them and then the area that is experiencing crisis. They will usually be more intensely motivated by the area, or areas, that they experienced the most lack in during their own formidable years of life. People who grew up poor may have an overwhelming desire to never be poor again. Those who had a bad family environment will desire a better family experience for themselves. People who had poor examples of health and fitness modeled to them will perhaps vow to never be that unhealthy.

The challenge is not so much the specific single life-value that was displayed most prominently to them; rather, it is the fact that one single life-value was displayed to them, period. They were taught to believe that you can only do one thing well. At least only one thing at a time.

So, a person who grows up in a good family (one-value) but experienced a lack of money will typically give inordinate amounts of attention and energy to making money, often at the expense of other pertinent life-values. As they're pouring themselves completely into their work and business, their home life eventually begins to unravel. Simply put, the script that was handed to them taught them to isolate a single value and attempt to rectify it without presenting a multi-valued matrix. Therefore, they think they've solved a generational problem of poverty. Then they wake up one day at 45 and realize that while they may have solved the poverty issue, they've created several other bigger problems.

Other values of your life are not going to give you a free pass just because you've worked hard in one area. The dysfunction just increases exponentially. While you're making money, your marriage is falling apart. While you're tending to the needs of a spouse and kids, you're missing opportunities to make more money. While you are working long hours to get ahead, you're gaining weight, stress, and anxiety. So, you disconnect from all social activity and friends so you can really pour into the problem areas of your life, end up losing the incredible value of connection, and the liability and dysfunction of one- or two-value success are perpetuated yet again. And it never occurs to most people that it is the synergy of equal growth and development that is the key to total life improvement. So, disconnecting from one area to address another one only weakens your ability to grow the one you are focusing on.

The question many would ask right about now is this: "How do you make something matter to you that has never mattered before?" And that's a very good and legitimate question. Developing values that were never modeled for you can be a daunting task. However, acknowledging your circle of values is the imperative first step in approaching your quest to "have it all."

More attention is given to this question in the next chapter, but for now, you must be willing to adopt new priorities. Some that you presently embrace will remain, but be sure, you will need to end up with some new priorities you currently may not have. Your values are your compass by which all your decisions, choices, and actions are measured. *Your values are your personal circle!*

You must come to a place where anything less than equal development and advancement in all seven life-values is unacceptable.

Most people's experience of trying to address one life-value at a time is a momentum thief at the very least. More often, it results in spending all your time putting out one small fire after another. Just about the time you get a little traction in one area, the bottom falls out of another. About the time you get things going smoothly on the job, the tension in the home becomes palpable. You get things settled at home with the family and your job is in jeopardy. You get some semblance of rhythm in those and realize it has cost you in your health or your social life has been diminished. The scenarios go on and on. This is precisely why the once popularly embraced concept of "compartmentalization" has long since been abandoned by behavioral and psychology experts.

> Just as your car runs more smoothly and requires less energy to go faster and farther when the wheels are in perfect alignment, you perform better when your thoughts, feelings, emotions, goals, and values are in balance.
> —Brian Tracy

The idea of compartmentalization may seem to serve as beneficial in extreme cases but only for a very short period, such as experiencing an extreme crisis or loss that makes you pull back a bit to address it. Or you start doing some internal work to heal childhood hurts and traumas and realize that you may have to deal with some issues one at a time. But most people find that the other values of life will not sit patiently waiting for you to get a single area dialed in.

In contrast, the other values of your circle will start screaming out for the same level of attention and focus you are giving to another. That's just the way the human experience works.

For this reason, you must learn practices and techniques to give equal amounts of time, effort, and attention to all areas simultaneously. Getting your life automated with effective patterns and habits is key to equally distributing your time, energy, attention, and focus to the entirety of your circle simultaneously. I want to help you achieve just that... a perfect balance within your circle so you can experience life the way it was meant to be experienced, *abundantly*!

Before we get into effective ways to strategize and execute a new plan to move you toward a life of joy, abundance, and fulfillment, let's break each of the seven values down individually. The next several chapters are the seven single values that you will have to learn to collectively develop and manage. These make up your circle.

2

THE QUEST FOR SPIRITUALITY

(SPIRITUAL VALUE)

I AM A MAN OF FAITH, PRAYER, AND REGULAR church attendance. So, I have no negative aversions to being committed to God in the context of religious activity. But I'd like to take you into a discussion that simply transcends a particular confession or church attendance alone. It is a conversation about pursuing God with a sense of awe and purpose and the incredible clarity of significance that grows out of that. This is critical to the building of your circle.

It is true that when one gets their spiritual life really dialed in, everything else seems to follow suit more easily. However, it is certainly not automatic.

Religion is generally defined as an identification with an established tradition of a particular faith or doctrine, centered around the sacred or an otherwise supernatural deity. But one must be diligent to not allow their devotion toward God to become simply perfunctory.

A healthy spiritual life is one that is aligned with God so closely that His divine attributes start showing up in your life: **generosity, giving, significance, creativity, honor, a respect, and appreciation for all of life, and a love for people.** All these attributes become amazingly relevant and needed to develop and grow the other values in your circle.

A real spiritual pursuit of God is when you, as an individual, get aligned with your highest purpose and calling that is transcendent of all other aspects of your life. It is when you are constantly in awe of God and His greatness, His faithfulness, His mercy, and His love.

YOUR HIGHEST CALLING

There is tremendous understanding in looking at the Genesis account of the first known man, Adam. When God created Adam and placed him in the Garden of Eden, he was first engaged in the daily habit of being in intimate fellowship with God. Scripture tells us that Adam met with God every day at a specific time and communed — or had fellowship — with God. He walked around the Garden of Eden with a sense of awe concerning God's handiwork. That's saying something. The instructions (or assignment) to tend to the garden, dress it, and have dominion over the earth came out of that. However, the foremost and highest calling in a person's life is to be a follower and a pursuer of God.

We often get confused over purpose and calling and then assignment and gifting. Whatever it is you do in the context of church or spiritual activity is not a substitute for your purpose. Let me explain it this way:

I serve as a staff pastor in a great church in Houston Texas. But I am not called to be a pastor. That is part of my current assignment. I am called to pursue God and then lead my family to do the same. As I do that, I gain clarity concerning what it is God has assigned me to do. I then discover that the gifting in my life is compatible with and conducive to my assignment.

Never confuse what you are assigned to do with what you are called to do. If you do not yet know what it is that you are specifically assigned to do, you need not worry. As you commit yourself to follow God through prayer, devotion, and worship with all of your being, your assignment will find you.

King David spent the early years of his life out in the pastures of his father, tending to flocks of sheep. Many of the psalms were written during that time. David was able to spend his life as a worshipper of God. As he grew in this dimension of his life, things started to unfold.

The prophet Samuel was given instructions by God to go to the house of Jesse, David's father, and anoint the next king of Israel. After God passed over all of David's brothers, Samuel had Jesse call for the most unlikely candidate, David. And when he walked into the house, God spoke to Samuel and said, "This is the one, anoint him… and send him to the palace to start serving." You see, instructions, or your assignment, will find you when you are committed to and engaged in your calling.

Years later, David had apparently gotten so enamored with his gifting and assignment that he drifted from his purpose. His whole life began to unravel as a result. Again, whatever it is that you do can never be a replacement for what you are! You are called to be an intimate worshipper of God.

It is easy for all of us to drift from our purpose when we worry too much about the needs and desires we have for our lives. We want to build a business, succeed in a career, make some money, have some nice things, etc. We all have goals and dreams that we give ourselves to. But Christ put all of that into perspective for us when he said, "But seek ye first the kingdom of God, and his righteousness; and all these things shall be added unto you" (Matt. 6:33). The question is understandable: what are "all these other things?"

The preceding verses should liberate you from this worry. Christ informs us of "what things" he is referring to in verses 31 and 32: "Therefore take no thought, saying, what shall we eat? or, what shall we drink? or, wherewithal shall we be clothed? (For after all these things do the Gentiles seek.) For your heavenly Father knows that ye have need of all these things."

Simply put, God knows you have real needs, desires, concerns, goals, etc. And it's interesting that Jesus acknowledges them as "needs." The issue isn't that God wants you to forget about ever having anything, accomplishing anything, or becoming anything. Rather, the principle is that when you are committed to your highest purpose and calling—to seek after God—all the other "stuff" will find you.

YOUR CALLING/PURPOSE IS INHERENT.

There is an aspect of human nature, a prominent one, that seeks the eternal. Something within all of us that peaks our interest, stirs within our appetites, and constantly pulls on us, to in turn reach out to embrace it. It is an intrinsic desire to discover and experience our truest and best self, embedded in something greater than that self. Or an individual connectedness and oneness with a transcendent being greater than ourselves. Ecclesiastes 3:11 says it this way: "He has made everything beautiful in its time. *He has also set eternity in the human heart.*"

God himself has placed within each of us an inherent curiosity and awareness of the existence of God and our need of Him.

The Christian's view of God is that He is not impersonal or simply a supreme consciousness, in which one loses his or her individuality when united with the Divine—but because God is a relational being within Himself (a holy Trinity), relationship or union with this triune God makes it possible to both lose yourself in something bigger than you and subsequently find your greater authentic self. I think that is amazingly beautiful.

God's own distinctiveness ensures that our individuality or identity is not obliterated because of coming into union with Him. Rather, it results in a greater discovery of ourselves in conjunction with a deeper discovery of Him. Christ, in fact, regularly taught his disciples to lose themselves in order that they might find themselves.

Regardless of your personal experiences with specific churches, organizations, or faith groups, a healthy insatiable pursuit of God should be your highest priority for many reasons.

As food, water, and sleep is imperative to your physical health… so the pursuit of God is to your purpose, identity, morality, affirmations, and so forth.

Pursuing God allows us to come to a place of neutrality, free from hurt, offenses, and negative exposure, so we can look at life and our relationship to it through the lens of hope and possibility... and not through a lens marred by past hurts and experiences.

The pursuit of God brings greater clarity to your character and conduct. Your character, whether good or bad, cannot be solely the result of influences that are themselves, temporal and limited. Worthy values are moral, communal, and timeless. This is *such* great news because it means that your character isn't helplessly determined by experiences and external achievements or failures. You can change your character when you are connecting with a God who transcends all those things.

The clarity and purity of values have a standard that is universally applicable. Simply, lying is wrong regardless of culture, geography, or your personal feeling. Stealing would be the same. Cheating will, yet again, be the same. The pursuit of God takes your observations and self-reflection of values outside of culture and clique. When God is the standard of evaluation, it breeds a togetherness between all of us as human beings.

Has it ever occurred to you that 100 pianos all tuned to the same fork are automatically tuned to each other? They are of one accord by being tuned, not to each other, but to another standard to which each one must individually bow.

–A. W. Tozer

There must be something you espouse to that is higher than and outside of you—for all those times when you come to the end of yourself. The fact that we have as many versions of what is good or evil as there are people on the earth is the result of having as many standards as possible of measurement.

The pursuit of God gives you a more productive standard for self-reflection and examination. Constructive reflection and self-examination are virtues of true spirituality. We typically measure ourselves by the context we are surrounded by; other people, societal standards and expectations, the wealth of others, the accomplishments of our friends, etc.

There are certainly benefits to "comparison" when it comes to productivity and progress. But not so when it comes to value and self-worth. It is far more beneficial in these areas to assess yourself as one who is embedded in, or who exists in, the Divine, whose unchanging perspective of you is one of unconditional love and acceptance.

> The unexamined life is
> not worth living.
>
> —Socrates

DON'T FEAR THE FUEL THAT EMPOWERS YOU.

The lack of interest or motivation in pursuing God seems to be the concern that we innately associate the concepts of sacrifice, pain, selflessness, humility, and relinquishing certain aspects of our ego to actively pursue God. However, these are the same experiences most often connected to personal growth of any kind. To succeed at anything will require you to exercise a certain amount of sacrifice, discipline, and delayed gratification. Therefore, the pursuit of God results in the very things that will contribute to growth in the totality of your life.

You don't need to pursue God in the context of a single-value consideration, thereby repeating the futility of single-value success. Meaning, I don't suggest that you go live in a cave, move to a monastery, take a vow of poverty, or commit to a miserable life of isolation and complete solitude. It doesn't help you or anybody else to be super spiritual and broke, addicted, or a loner.

Instead, learn to see God in your everyday life through the lens of healthy spirituality. God is everywhere and in everything. He has a supernatural ability to work things for your good regardless of their severity. Pursue Him. Put Him first. Give a voice to the sense of eternity within you. This is your purpose. The other stuff comes easy when He is first.

THE AWE FACTOR

What we need to do is learn "the science of awe." Something that makes you tremble, makes your knees weak—an awareness that jolts your perspective—you are being cared for, watched, and guided by a force that is greater than you.

Only recently have scientists begun to study the inseparable correlation between the awe factor and spirituality.

For instance, in a recent experiment to study the correlation between the "awe factor" and spirituality, scientists randomly assigned study participants to view one of three things:

1. A five-minute video of the BBC's *Planet Earth*, consisting of stunning footage of vast plains, mountains, canyons, the ocean, and space.
2. A five-minute video of the BBC's *Walk on the Wild Side*, intended to be amusing.
3. A 1959 news interview conducted by Mike Wallace.

Not so surprisingly, after their viewing, individuals who watched the *Planet Earth* segment expressed a greater belief that the universe is controlled by God or other supernatural forces, as well as a stronger belief in God more generally, than those in the other two conditions.

In the end, it was the self-transcendent emotions that individuals experienced, such as "awe," that played the biggest role in accounting for the positive link found between spirituality and well-being.

You need to be still, get quiet, and experience the awe of God's love for you. See His magnificent handiwork in nature. See Him in the birth of a child. Consider the vastness of the universe. If you are looking and opening your heart and mind to Him, you'll see Him everywhere, and it will keep you in awe.

The Christian's view was found to be quite contributory to experiencing awe: the idea that God has revealed Himself in bodily form in the person of Jesus Christ. The beliefs that correspond with this are best said by the apostle Paul in 1 Timothy 3:16. "Without question, this is the great mystery of our faith: Christ was revealed in a human body and vindicated by the Spirit. He was seen by angels and announced to the nations. He was believed in throughout the world and taken to heaven in glory."

These beliefs transcend logic, human reasoning, and natural order thinking to such a degree that one cannot help but be in awe of them.

The pursuit of God should lead you down paths that fill you with awe. A healthy pursuit of God should never result in stagnation or boredom. Neither should it create any kind of plateau. That's what religion by itself will do. But staying engaged in an intimate pursuit of God will result in an exponentially evolving awareness of the awesomeness of God.

I find it interesting that the angels that are the very closest to the throne of God—or the place of His concentrated presence—are described as being full of eyes from their heads to their toes. (Ezek. 10:12) That seems odd... until we consider that the scriptures also teach us that our eyes are the windows through which revelation enters our hearts and souls (Matt. 6:22–23).

These angels are so exposed to eternal volumes of the revelation of God that one pair of eyes isn't enough. They are full of eyes, and they need all of them. They are recorded in both the Old and New Testaments as proclaiming the words "holy, holy, holy" constantly, for thousands of years.

Many Jewish theologians believe that every time they proclaim "holy, holy, holy," it is in response to a new discovery or revelation about God. This is what a genuine, unpretentious, and authentic pursuit of God should do. The closer you get to Him and the more you discover about

Him, the more you realize that you know so little about Him, yet you want to pursue Him even more.

FAITH IS ROOTED IN SPIRITUALITY.

The irony is that the very thing necessary for the pursuit of God is the same that, itself, emanates *from* God. Faith is extremely important in one's life. Hebrews 11:1 defines faith as "confidence in what we hope for and assurance about what we cannot see."

If you take the purely scientific approach to life, in which everything is established through observation, measurement, and experience before it can be factual, your quest for completeness will be significantly stymied.

There will always be certain realities that fall outside of those boundaries that you will have to embrace with conviction and vigor. Situations that will require you to suspend reason and logic and believe something on an entirely different basis. That is faith.

No one ever progressed beyond ordinary to the realms of the extraordinary without having to constantly exercise pure and raw faith… believing in something—a possibility, a hope, a dream—just because there was something unexplainable in your heart that you couldn't articulate but that made you believe it was true or at least possible. This is the very quality that helps us to believe in a power greater than ourselves.

Qualities necessary to accomplish big things—creativity, innovation, and believing in the impossible—are divine traits that exist within us all. The pursuit of God will give these qualities wings quicker than anything.

Beyond believing that God exists, you will live a life in which you are stretched beyond reason and challenged far beyond logic. You will be provoked by God to believe that something that never was is totally possible. Not just *in* His existence but in the potential of people, the achievement of dreams, the irrelevance of limitations, and that the boundaries established by the failures of others are only temporary.

> The **reasonable** man **adapts** himself to the **world**; the **unreasonable** one **persists** in trying to **adapt** the **world** to himself. **Therefore, all progress** depends on the **unreasonable** man.
>
> –George Bernard Shaw

The fact is that every great thing, idea, invention, or technology was at one time considered to be impossible and even a ridiculous notion. Until someone ordinary came along and dared to endure ridicule, scorn, humiliation from others, and the disappointment of failing a few times, to bring into existence something that never was.

Faith is not far from you. Powerful faith comes to us intertwined with the Divine words already written (scripture) and the words or impressions God speaks presently to us from within. I'm not going to overcomplicate this with an exhaustive explanation. Let's keep it simple—when you hear Divine words, whether through teaching, exhortation and encouragement, internal impressions, or your own reading of scripture, faith builds and increases significantly within you. That's it!

Don't be paralyzed by overanalyzing everything on the front end. Just pursue God daily through prayer, meditation of scripture, and music and songs to Him. Listen to Him. Shut out the thundering noise of life, other people's opinions, and your own scattered thoughts. Ask God for guidance and direction from within. Nurture the sense of awe regarding Him. See Him everywhere and in everything. Spend regular time with Him. Have an ongoing conversation between you and Him that doesn't end.

When He is the primary purpose of your life you will become clearer on your assignment. You will have a better handle on the things you should "do" in your life. All of your dreams, goals, and desires are out there looking for you. They've simply been instructed to chase down the people who are fulfilling their highest call!

3

MASTERING YOUR EMOTIONS

(EMOTIONAL VALUE)

IN MANY WAYS, THE DIGITAL EXPERIENCE HAS taken over our lives and provided us with a pseudo-social experience and no preparation for real, legitimate emotions. Education centers around competitive needs such as technology, science, etc., and literally *no* preparation for emotional management. Through social media platforms, we instantly gain a whole community of friends and lose them just as quickly. Simply follow or unfollow. And we do so without too much emotional investment or loss. It's simply "meh."

Emotional mastery has always been necessary, but now, with significantly more adversity, the need is even greater. Our culture's social construct is becoming void of human emotion and real authentic feelings, but that doesn't change the internal wirings of the human experience. We are communal beings. We desire to live in tribes, interact in meaningful ways, and grow as people because of those interactions. And there are valuable factors that come into play in these types of scenarios:

How we respond to ideas and experiences that are contrary to our preferences. How to cope with sudden anxieties. How to process life surrounded by so many uncertainties. And of course, how to manage our emotions. These all add greatly to the development of character within your circle.

I think you would agree that technology, trends, cultural dynamics, and the like have far surpassed our emotional preparedness. And the tragedy of it is that opportunities, careers, families, meaningful relationships, business deals, etc. are most often sabotaged because someone didn't control their emotions during a moment when it was critical to do so.

In my theological studies, I have been intrigued by the stringent requirements placed on ancient Jewish priests concerning the management of their emotions. History as well as scripture tell us that ancient Jewish priests who performed duties inside the first chamber of the temple were permitted to mourn for the dead for seven days. Then they were to wash their faces, change their clothes, and be strong in front of the people.

Further instructions were given to those priests that went into the deeper chambers of the temple, to limit their periods of mourning to three days. Still further, the High Priests who performed the sacred, once-a-year ritual inside the holiest of places had to limit their mourning to one day.

And if that wasn't demanding enough, there's a particular case in which, according to scripture, a certain prophet named Ezekiel was told by God that before the morning, his wife was going to die. He was told to mourn that night because when the morning came, he wasn't going to be permitted to mourn at all. He would have to stand in front of the nation and display strong leadership and guidance.

That may seem extreme or insensitive, but there are a few incredibly valuable principles to draw out:

1. The more elevated position or influence one has, the more critical it is that they are absolutely in control of their emotions.

2. Conversely, the more in control you are of your emotions, the more you are likely to experience elevation in your life.

In hindsight, I have learned something from my father. However insensitive it may seem or whether it was the ideal parenting model or not is irrelevant to me today. My father taught me some extremely valuable lessons when it came to my emotional response to things. His method was simple… when my conduct or rebellion deserved punishment, it came in twos. I would get a woópin' (no, not a spanking, but a woopin') for whatever disobedience I had committed. Then, he would count to ten and say, "Now, dry those eyes and stop your crying, or you'll get some more." The lesson was simple. It isn't the things that happen to us in life that derail our progress nearly as much as it is our reaction to those things.

Sometimes life is hard. Marriages are stressful. We have disagreements with people close to us. The world breeds anxiety and our loved ones disappoint us. That's all completely normal. But marriages have been irretrievably damaged, businesses sabotaged, relationships destroyed, and incredible opportunities have been squandered, not because of some measure of crisis or difficulty—rather, somebody didn't control their emotions. Therefore, they reacted in a way that was counterproductive to success. Words were spoken out of ramped-up emotions, decisions were made when uncontrolled feelings trumped sensibility, and good patterns were broken because of a fleeting emotion that wasn't kept in check.

I love what Tony Robbins and other behavioral specialists have referred to as the "triad of emotions."

Mastering your own emotions may seem next to impossible initially. Most people are under the impression that their emotional makeup is entirely genetic. "I'm just wired this way." "If you met my father or mother, you'd understand why I'm like this." Or as was my own personal excuse… "The Miller blood just runs hot!"

NATURE OR NURTURE

What helped and continues to help me is the awareness that the difference between nature and nurture is very significant and impactful. By nature, I mean genetics. I'm 5' 11"... that's genetic. I have blue eyes... that's genetic. My bone structure is heavy and dense... that's genetic. But being 5' 11", blue-eyed, and stout doesn't particularly determine my degree of success. It's the things I learned by nurturing that have played a far more significant role in how things have gone in my life.

Methods of conflict resolution, vocal tone, mannerisms of speaking, knee-jerk reactions, and life perspectives—however natural they felt to me—were in fact the product of long-term exposure to a certain environment. An environment where all these things were absorbed. Meaning, even my emotional makeup is largely the result of nurturing rather than inherent wiring that I can't be held responsible for.

Not everything that contributed to my emotional makeup was my fault. In fact, most of it was beyond my own doing. But there's a big difference between accepting the blame and taking responsibility. The simple fact is that I am completely responsible for the man I am today and the one I continue to evolve into.

The good news is simply stated but of great magnitude in its application... *in the same way you learned these things, you can re-learn new ones.*

No one ever said it was easy, but you can teach yourself how to be a master of your own emotions if you adhere to some basic disciplines. Start by paying attention to the triad of emotional management model. Three factors that you are in total control of.

PHYSIOLOGY

The difference between talking with your fists clenched and your teeth gritted as opposed to not is quite substantial. Pay attention to your physical posture when you are experiencing movement in your emotions.

Specific neurological functions within our brain are responsible for certain factors as a response to perceived threats or disruptions to our well-being. An elevated heart rate, the tension of muscles, blood pressure rising, rate of breathing increasing, and bursts of energy that may last for several minutes. These are but some of the things we physically encounter at times. In other words, our brains are wired in such a way as to influence us to act before we can properly consider the consequences of our actions.

Intentional physiology becomes quite critical in managing the effects of these natural body functions. The more you can learn to regulate these factors, the greater chance you'll have to make good judgments and decisions.

Picture two guys arguing: chest to chest, nose to nose. Their volume continues to increase. They are both standing there with fists clenched ready to go. In just a matter of time, this is going to escalate into an explosive physical altercation. How dramatically different would this scenario turn out if one of these men made a choice to de-escalate the situation by simply sitting down? Quite differently, I imagine.

Every emotion has a corresponding physical expression. You can either be defensive or proactive with it. Open your fists and your teeth; you'll relieve tension. Breathe slower and deeper and walk around a bit; you'll clear your thoughts and reset your mood. Stand up straight; you'll feel more confident. Do whatever you have to do to regulate the effects in your body as well as limit their role in choosing what you say and do.

FOCUS

Whatever you focus on captures your energy. When you focus on the things that are wrong, what you don't have, who's holding you back, and a host of other negative directions, your energy will drain out of you. Where you direct your focus determines your intentions. Every one of your internal systems follows your intentions. I love what the book of Proverbs says: "Let your eyes look straight ahead; fix your gaze directly before you."

This is one of the ways you control the internal narrative that goes on in your head. All of us have these ongoing conversations, or narratives, within ourselves. Those are the most important conversations you'll ever have. Because at the end of the day, you will either persuade yourself toward completeness or you'll talk yourself out of it.

One of my favorite "guiding" scriptures is in the epistle to the Philippians: "Finally, brothers and sisters, whatever is true, whatever is noble, whatever is right, whatever is pure, whatever is lovely, whatever is admirable—if anything is excellent or praiseworthy—think about such things" (Phil. 4:8).

If you focus on how things once were, you will miss out on how things can be. If you focus on lack, scarcity, revenge, regret, etc., you'll get more of the same. But that's not what you want. You want the "complete life." And that's what you are becoming... complete! So you cannot gaze at what everyone else is. You must keep looking at the things that no one else can see now. And in time, you'll have what few others have!

LANGUAGE

For centuries, experts have operated on the assumption that language was relegated to being expressive or reflective of our emotions. Only in recent decades has the psychological community begun seeing the power of language to assist in managing emotions rather than just describing them after the fact. In other words, our language has a lot more power than simply describing what we are feeling. Our words have the power to create perception or give new meaning to an emotion and even reshape its nature.

Greatly simplified... you may not be able to completely control your breathing, heart rate, blood pressure, muscle tension, or the bursts of energy from elevating, but by your language, you can determine what it all means and how you'll respond to it. It's a powerful tool to use to take control of that internal commentator that just never shuts up.

Every one of us needs to be a builder of our own vocabulary. We need to commit to language that avoids words that incite negativity and escalate situations unnecessarily. We've all said them:

- *You know what your problem is...* puts you in a position of being arrogant and judgmental and puts the person you're talking to immediately on the defensive.
- *You always...* really? Always—as in every single time? You get the point.
- *With all due respect...* usually means you're getting ready to throw respect out the window and give them a piece of your mind.
- *Well, it is what it is...* usually means you're not taking responsibility or you're deeming a fixable situation as unfixable.
- *What's wrong with you...* you're already assuming something's wrong with them and not open to the possibility that there may be something wrong with you.
- And on and on...

And these are just words and phrases that we inadvertently say without considering their effect on others. What about our own "self-talk." Apostle Paul says in Ephesians 4:29, "Let no corrupt talk come out of your mouths, but only such as is good for building up, as fits the occasion, that it may give grace to those who hear." But it doesn't specify that this only applies to the impact of your words on others.

The most important conversation in your life is the ongoing one that you have with yourself. Ask yourself the questions: "Are there specific words that I use often that provoke negative emotions in me?" "What are the words that reinforce limitations?" What do I regularly say that supports insecurity and a negative complex?" Write these words down, cross them out when you have replaced every single one of them with words that incite vision, faith, hope, clarity, and confidence.

Do the same thing with the words you often say to others. Replace those words with ones that nurture great communication. Words that make others believe in themselves. Ones that cause others to blossom because of conversing with you.

The process of managing your circle demands that you evaluate your vocabulary and assess the impact of your words, whether positive or negative. In the middle of an emotional escalation is not the most ideal time to try and do this. A person in pursuit of completeness must discipline their vocabulary and always stick to it and in all circumstances. Someone once said, "Be sure to taste your own words before you spit them out."

> Vocabulary is a matter of word-building as well as word-using.
>
> –David Crystal

Language patterns and phraseology are easier to correct than you might think. It just takes some analysis and a commitment to change it.

Scott Adams said, "Your inability to see other possibilities and your lack of vocabulary are your brain's limits, not the universe's."

Since we know that if you want to change your life you must change your mind, and thoughts are the results of words (or words create thoughts), then a better way to say the former would be: "If you want to change your life, change your vocabulary." If you want to change other people's lives, then make your vocabulary something others gravitate to.

The apostle James communicates (Jas. 3:2–10) two analogies to describe the power and potential of our vocabulary:

1. The small rudders of great ships.
2. The tiny bits we put into a horse's mouth.

By both analogies, we know that the words we say have the power to produce life, build dreams, edify people, and elevate the trajectory of everyone around us. Adversely, we can also tear down and destroy with the same. Whatever principle we take from all this concerning how we talk to others is equally applicable to how we talk to ourselves.

In summary, your emotions are the body's reaction to the activity of your mind. Take control of your vocabulary, and you'll take control of your mind. Take control of your mind and you'll get control of your emotions.

4

GROW YOUR INTELLECT

(COGNITIVE VALUE)

INTELLECTUAL DEVELOPMENT REFERS TO THE changes that occur because of growth and experience in a person's capacities for thinking, reasoning, relating, judging, and conceptualizing. It's becoming psychologically well. Nurturing your capacity to learn and grow. It also encompasses the will of a person and the ability to make choices freely, all of which is critical when it comes to the aspect of self-mastery.

First, the argument as to how critical the role of the intellect is to being a complete person. Most people seem to be polarized by one of two extreme views (both of which need to be avoided): *rationalism* and *anti-intellectualism.*

The rationalist believes that, given enough time, one can always "figure things out" for themselves—that human intellect can surmount any problem. The mind of man can understand all reality, solving any problem, and producing whatever we need.

Anti-intellectualism is the rejection of reason as the remedy for all that is in the world. The anti-intellectualist downplays academic pursuits and instead promotes feelings, intuition, and spontaneous action as much more useful in engaging reality and solving problems.

As you might suspect, I'm going to suggest that there are bits of truth in each, but somewhere in the middle is the most productive place to be.

JUST BECAUSE YOU ARE DONE WITH YOUR PAST DOESN'T MEAN YOUR PAST IS DONE WITH YOU!

There are many articles, research projects, and scientifically validated studies that speak of both the attention that must be given to as well as the many benefits of intellectual and cognitive development in children. I contend, as do many others, that it never stops being equally imperative to develop and nurture intellectual growth. My mentor, Dr. Richard Heard, always said, "If you're not growing, you're dying."

In the realm of intellect, one must be careful not to fall into old thoughts, patterns, and ideas. You should avoid ever plateauing when it comes to intellectual development.

Yesterday's ideas and thought patterns carry the sting of yesterday's defeats and limitations.

To get stuck in your intellectual growth is the equivalent of resubmitting to the challenges and limitations of the past. Remember, just because you are done with your past doesn't mean your past is done with you. If you don't become intentional about increasing your cognitive and intellectual capacity, you will leave the power to shape your future in the possession of your past. And it is through a mind that isn't growing into a Christ-like maturity that your adversarial forces empower your past to keep working you over.

Your alignment with God will result in you being, as 2 Corinthians 5:17 says, "Therefore if any man be in Christ, he is a new creature: old things are passed away; behold, all things have become new."

However, just as this transformation requires great effort on your part to stay distanced from old habits and behaviors, it also requires great effort to feed and nurture your new mind.

Consider for a moment: We are told in 2 Peter 1:3–9,

> His divine power has given us everything we need for a godly life through our knowledge of Him who called us by His own glory and goodness. Through these, He has given us his very great and precious promises, so that through them you may participate in the divine nature, having escaped the corruption in the world caused by evil desires. For this very reason, make every effort to add to your faith goodness; and to goodness, knowledge; and to knowledge, self-control; and to self-control, perseverance; and to perseverance, godliness; and to godliness, mutual affection; and to mutual affection, love. For if you possess these qualities in increasing measure, they will keep you from being ineffective and unproductive in your knowledge of our Lord Jesus Christ. But whoever does not have them is nearsighted and blind, forgetting

that they have been cleansed from their past sins.

Think of that—the scriptures connect our ability to receive from God, His promises, and provisions, to our personal growth; including but not limited to, the growth of knowledge. And if we are to give credence to the order He writes them in, then we must accept that the most important thing to add to your life, after faith and goodness, is knowledge.

It has been stated that *the average man gravitates toward the mirror:* Meaning we tend to stay in areas, circumstances, social constructs, and routines that feel safe and familiar to us. One of the many problems with that is the fact that almost anything that God calls you into or challenges you with is going to require you to get uncomfortable. He will call you into unchartered territory or ask you to do something that is beyond your current capacity or ability. You must keep growing my friend!

So, you must see your intellectual capacity as an integral part of God's redemptive plan. This is how you will acquire new knowledge, understand hidden wisdom, dissect your behavior patterns, and discipline your ability to focus. Prayer and devotion to God are the imperative beginning. However, you must keep adding to that value.

No Olympic athlete ever just prayed their way into a gold medal. They may have prayed, but after they prayed, they got up early, ate right, trained hard, and kept on working when everyone else quit. That's what champions do. They pray, trust, and lean into God. Then, they put in the hard work and discipline to separate themselves from the pack, rise above the competition, and *win*! This is mental toughness. This is focus. This is what you must grow.

Great people, historically, are identified and set apart not so much for their physical prowess or brain IQ but by uncommon focus, courage, tenacity, and stickability. They set their minds to something and continue until the task is done. They assess what kind of habits, patterns, food, etc. are essential to their success as well as the liabilities that need to be eliminated. When that is determined, decisions are made, necessary changes are established, and they never look back. This is all part of the self-mastery to which we've been referring.

Times are changing, and the world continues to develop rapidly. To develop a full and complete life, the growth of your intellectual capacity must be a high value in your life.

No problem or challenge can be addressed from the same level of consciousness in which it was created.
–Albert Einstein

This is powerful on so many levels. There's a principle, shared by Napoleon Hill that states, *"All failure, all disappointment, and all adversity contain within itself the seed for an equal or greater benefit."* So, follow the logic here: if the seed for benefit and growth is contained within the problem in front of you, yet that problem can't be effectively addressed or solved at the level of cognitive consciousness that you are currently at, then growing your intellect becomes essential to your personal growth.

Growing your cognitive capacity is not a matter of reading and studying specific subjects only so you can become knowledgeable about that subject... it's about literally increasing your brain's capacity to work better and faster across the board.

Neural plasticity, or brain plasticity, is the brain's ability to form new neural connections, enabling you to function at a higher level. The more neural plasticity your brain has, the faster it makes new connections and the quicker and more effectively you process information. Since achieving significant success involves quick-thinking and sharp decision-making skills, it's alarming that so few train their brain accordingly. You should be addressing this matter daily.

The more knowledge and information you absorb, the more you have available to you from your intellectual reservoir. But absorbing knowledge, data, and information also increases the ability of your brain to work more quickly. This becomes invaluable in your decision-making as well as in your problem-solving abilities.

Learning will grow your confidence, increase your skill sets, and better equip you to take advantage of opportunities. It also allows you to be more innovative and creative in your work. It's always safe to assume there is more you can learn.

> You will be the same person five years from now as you are today, except for the people you meet and the books you read.
>
> –Charlie "Tremendous" Jones

GROW YOUR INTELLECT

There is a lot of research data available to anyone who is interested in increasing their cognitive capacity, but here are a few of my favorite things:

- Become a student of always learning.
- Read books and read them often.
- Have stimulating conversations with other people about real things that really matter.
- Ask thought-provoking questions and carry the dialogue through to a conclusion.
- Get plenty of aerobic exercise every day.
- Get plenty of sleep.
- Eat a lot of nutrient-rich foods.
- Take some online courses.
- Learn/practice a hobby.
- Play some memory games.

5

FIGHTING FOR YOUR FAMILY

(FAMILY VALUE)

THE HEALTH OF YOUR FAMILY RELATIONSHIPS matters a lot! Your family is your tribe. A place for you to be accepted as your true authentic self. Filled with people who love you unconditionally. A place where your ideals are shaped, challenged, and periodically assessed.

- A place of belonging, where we can learn to love.
- A place to learn interpersonal relationship skills.
- A place where we learn to practice selflessness, humility in serving, and preferring one another.
- A place where the ability to share the pursuit of others with them and help empower them to succeed is practiced.

Our past family relationships have helped to make each of us who we are as adults, and influence how we now treat our own children and other family members.

Brad Wilcox of the American Enterprise Institute, and the director of the National Marriage Project at the University of Virginia, published a study that found that

> ...states with more married parents do better on a broad range of economic indicators, including upward mobility for poor children and lower rates of child poverty. On most economic indicators, the percentage of parents who are married in a state is a better predictor of that state's economic health than the racial composition and educational attainment of the state's residents.

Even Princeton University and the Brookings Institution released a similar study reporting that "most scholars now agree that children raised by two biological parents in a stable marriage do better than children in other family forms across a wide range of outcomes."

I could cite page after page of research and study on the matter of family from some of the best learning institutions in the country. So why then is the subject of family such a controversial one, with as many ideas and opinions about it as there are people in the conversation?

Certainly not to oversimplify it, but perhaps because it is the ultimate prize that *the powers that be* are fighting for. From the day you were born, your identity, language, worldview, and expectations about how the world should work are shaped in the home. Consequently, the family as an institution ends up being far more important to the direction of a nation than even its government and institutions of education.

However, it's bigger than just that. Not having the wife and kids' context doesn't mean you can extract this value from your circle, nor does having had negative experiences growing up within your biological family. The character and skills learned and applied in that context are still imperative. You cannot neglect the idea of family because of a dysfunctional experience in the structure of your own biological family.

First, families have come to be represented in any number of ways:

- birth family
- family of marriage
- kinship family
- stepfamily
- blended family
- foster family
- adoptive family
- co-parenting family
- chosen family

These are all family structures that if we understand the value of such, offer a plethora of advantages and experiences we should learn to cherish. And while some take their greater comfort in small strategically self-constructed family groups, there are still many reasons why the family can be your best bet for life-relatable benefits:

1) OUR FAMILIES ARE THE BEST CONTEXT IN WHICH TO ACQUIRE VALUABLE SKILLS THAT MOST RESEMBLE REAL LIFE.

The close and tight-knit group of people that you may have committed to do life with perhaps have become more like family to you than your own. But there are certain facts that just don't change. Whether the experiences were positive or negative, most studies tell us that the experiences acquired in our biological family environment have far deeper roots in our lives and yield far more consequences as well.

These other groups of people may certainly add value to your life experience, but they still do not reflect some of the valuable factors posed by the family unit of your upbringing. Such as generational diversity, temperament differences, and a premise for self-worth, to name a few.

The concern we should have about negating the families we grew up in, in exchange for our own constructed groups of people we call our families, is that these constructed groups are typically made up of other people most like us.

Every generation drifts toward the mirror... the ease of likeness and similarity will always pull on us over the beauty of diversity. We tend to be a forgetful people.

We usually will not have people in our group-family that are hard to get along with or share extremely juxtaposed opinions, have significant age gaps, have differing world views, etc. Therefore, the ability to accommodate and navigate among such diversities remains largely undeveloped.

In our families, we can experience Grandma's funeral arrangements, Uncle Fred's political views rooted in the 1970s, our older cousin's plans when he turns twenty-one, our peer cousin's anguish over their inept soccer coach, school exams, and the poopie diapers and spoon feeding of our little nephew—all in one Saturday evening at the house.

Rather than simply endure it all, there's a subconscious increase in our capacity that beneficially spills over into the larger applications of our whole life-circle. That's one of the dependable nightmares, but also profound blessings, of being in our families. We get forced to spend time around people we would otherwise never have known about, wanted to meet, or thought we could get along with. And we are far better for it.

2) WE EXPERIENCE AND LEARN THE MOST BENEFICIAL IDEAL OF HEALTHY NEPOTISM.

Nepotism lays the groundwork of principle through which we experience unconditional love and self-worth based on a deeper reality rather than merit or demerit. It may be difficult to buy into there being any positive value in nepotism. Perhaps the only context and/or reference most of us have as an association or experience is anything but positive; however, let us dive a bit deeper into the conversation.

Historically, the idea of nepotism in Europe was particularly associated with the Catholic Church during the Renaissance and was not viewed very favorably. The term comes from the Italian word *nepotismo*, which is based on the Latin root *nepos*, meaning nephew. All through the late

17th century, numerous popes, and bishops, who had taken vows of celibacy and therefore had no legitimate offspring of their own, gave their nephews positions of leadership, which were often accorded by fathers to sons. The word nepotism was born when a series of Popes took to appointing their nephews, along with other family members, to top positions irrespective of their qualifications or talents.

To the masses, this was appalling and unfair. But you must separate yourself from the professional consideration of nepotism and see it as a great emotional antidote.

Think about it: We have all inescapably been the beneficiaries of the highest form of nepotism already. When we were born, we were one of millions of other babies also born. Yet our parents and family immediately took us home from the hospital, cared for us, pampered us, and fussed over us from day one. They spent money and extraordinary amounts of time, made substantial sacrifices and life adjustments for us… all because we belonged to the family. We hadn't achieved anything. We had done nothing deserving to merit such attention and devotion. We couldn't even talk or feed ourselves at that point.

Nepotism is what guarantees that our temper tantrums will be forgiven, and our bad days overlooked. It promises that we'll be supported throughout and despite our many disappointments. It is also what ensures that grown children will still attend Christmas and Thanksgiving dinners to celebrate with parents that may have done a less-than-stellar job themselves. Just because they're *our* parents. Sort of like the adage "blood is thicker than water."

We are all trying to forge our way ahead in a world where we are constantly evaluated based on productivity, achievement, and merit. Every one of us needs a basis for acceptance and love that is undeserved and without merit. A place where we know we won't be kicked out or rejected even when we have been a disappointment and gone through times of failure. Our families and homes provide as much.

Good leadership and humility will enable you to nurture even broken home situations and still allow you to reap the benefits and experience the advantages of the family. Bottom line... enjoy your friends and grow your personal communities, but don't give up on your family!

You don't have to do so at the neglect of all other life values, but in addition, fight for your family, even in the most dysfunctional of situations. The rewards for you are potentially fantastic.

3) OUR FAMILIES PROVIDE APPRECIATION AND NURTURING FOR OUR UNIQUENESS.

We live in a relatively cruel world where standards and norms are determined by entities and powers that really have no business telling any of us what is normal. Trends and fads change as often as the weather. What was once portrayed by artists as the optimal physical body of a woman 100 years ago would be called obese by the bougie fashion elites today. Length of hair, style, clothing choices, taste in music, and political views become the standard of the day. Culture dictates what is acceptable or even celebrated. And the price to pay for deviating from its declarations can be extremely costly. Costly to your own personal value, confidence, and your overall self-image.

The beauty of our families is that not only is it a safe place to be ourselves, but because we are among people that know who we really are deep inside, most often our uniqueness's will be celebrated. To the people that love us, being our unique selves is a luxury we can enjoy without cost.

6

INTENTIONAL ASSOCIATIONS

(SOCIAL VALUE)

LIFE MOVES AT THE SPEED OF RELATIONSHIPS and reflects the quality of those relationships. Your social value involves more thought and strategic consideration than the family you were born into. Your social circles consist of the people you choose and, while adding a different value than your family, are just as important as the value of family. Like any of the other values of your circle, they are critical to the success of the totality of your life.

Relationships are wonderful and add a great deal of color and value to your life, but they are difficult and sometimes messy as well. They require a great deal of work. Work, however, that will always pay great dividends eventually.

It is a long-held belief that a form of "symbiotic" living is a necessary component for humans to experience real growth and development. Not just a group of friends to hang out with, but groups wherein we intimately exist and participate in. Groups that may center around mutual interests, life themes, and other common denominators that serve as a source of challenge to aid in our development and growth.

We are not wired to flourish in our lives when we try to live like lone rangers. We are a tribal or communal species. We are our best when we interact with others of our species. Being introverted may make it slightly more difficult for you to engage in a social circle but not impossible. You just must work a little harder for it. But being antisocial means, you have an outright aversion to being around other people at all. This could be the Achilles heel of your success.

Social networking websites such as Instagram, Facebook, and others are popular today because they connect like-minded people through groups, interests, and subject forums. However, don't let a digital community reduce your evaluation of relationships to amassing contacts, acquiring "friends," or monitoring the daily posts of other people's lives. You need real-life social circles that demand more engagement and commitment from you than just a periodic post.

It is critical to your development and success to have social circles to which you belong. But it is equally critical that they are the right ones for you. Your social circle has a great deal of inadvertent influence on the life you lead and the people you meet. A good social circle can be accepting and open. However, a dysfunctional one can cause major personal and professional setbacks in your life.

Building a healthy and productive social circle is therefore very important. You should surround yourself with people who challenge you to be and do better. People whose company you enjoy and those to whom you can contribute as well.

But you need to be more specific in knowing who these people are and where they fit in your life. Nothing can drain you faster and even compromise the close relationships you do have in your life, like trying to nurture more than your capacity. The identification of where people are in your life matters greatly. It affects your time management, the quality of your contribution to others, and your own personal well-being.

Social scientists tell us that the average person only has the capacity to handle a broad circle of acquaintances of about 150 people. That's it. Further, your circle of preferred people will reduce to 15–20. But the magic social circle number seems to be five. Meaning, you will get your greatest amount of satisfaction from a tight-knit group of about five.

YOUR COMMUNITY-AT-LARGE CIRCLE

According to anthropologist Robin Dunbar, we have a biological limit of maintaining around 150 social interactions at the same time, with day-to-day interactions at about 50. These will be the people you invite to birthday parties, weddings, baby showers, holiday picnics, and backyard barbecues.

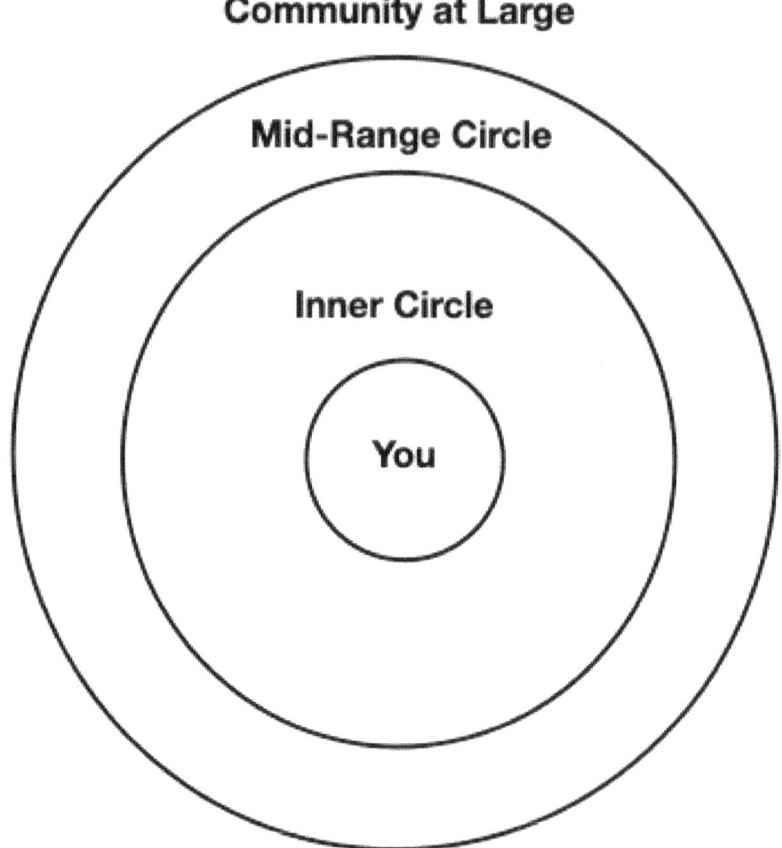

MID-RANGE CIRCLE

Fifteen to twenty. People you'd like to know more about and get to know better as opportunities afford. They're meaningful relationships but you won't remember their birthdays or anniversaries necessarily.

INTENTIONAL ASSOCIATIONS

INNER SOCIAL CIRCLE

Five. The people you want to spend the most time with. You remember the most important dates and details about their lives. These are the ones you'll make significant sacrifices for, walk with them through dark times, and want to share your life with.

You can't really go out tomorrow and staff the three primary communal circles of your life. They need to occur somewhat organically. However, if you can see the lack of clarity in your social life construct, then try this exercise:

Start by writing down the names of the people in your life. If you already know where they belong in your social circle construct, then put them there. Remember, the relationships in your mid-range circle and community at large will be a bit more fluid than your inner circle. Time, family responsibilities, job transfers, etc. will move people around some. Don't worry about all of that. Let it ebb and flow as it may. Just be there when you can and value the level of relationship you have with them when you have it.

However, you should be more purposeful about your inner circle. It should be just as important to you that you add as much value to them as you hope they contribute to you. "A man that has friends must show himself to be a friend" (Prov. 18:24).

Your well-defined social circle will additionally help you better manage your distribution of time and availability. You may be the kind of person that is always willing to fully help anyone in need of your ability—but that characteristic needs some discretion. Not everybody can have the same kind of access to you. Not everyone will know how to value it. Even Jesus was careful to steward the time and access He gave to those who were only there for what He could do for them, without any commitment on their part. "But Jesus, on His part, was not entrusting Himself to them, because He knew all people, and because He did not need anyone to testify about mankind, for He Himself knew what was in mankind" (John 2:24–25 NASB).

For years I have personally categorized the relationships in my life—outside of my immediate family—into three general groups. These are my peers, my mentors, and my mentees. I realize this may sound a little bougie, but it has probably saved me a lot of heartache and wasted time often. Here are my general rules of conduct for each:

PEERS

These are the people who are generally at the same place in life that I am. Among my peers, we can debate ideas, compare strategies, and jockey for the most time and influence among each other (slightly poking fun). We are all trying to get it worked out. Each of our ideas and opinions is just as likely to be true as the next.

MENTORS

These are the people who are already where I'm still trying to get. Among my mentors, I talk less and listen more. They have more to say than I do. I don't show up late for meetings, nor do I show up empty-handed. I'm not advocating that you need to write a check every time you connect with your mentor, but in terms of attentiveness, respect, conduct, and honor, you should always show them that you value the time and access they have given you.

MENTEES

These are the people who are still trying to reach what I have already conquered. I usually articulate to them the same rules I commit to concerning my attitude toward my mentors. Listen more and talk less. I know more than they do, thus, I have more to say than they do. They don't get to argue with me. Walk through some things first. Experience some failures, conquer a few things, and survive what I have, then we can debate.

Hopefully these variations of the social construct of your life will inspire you to be proactive in building a personal community of relationships that are mutually beneficial in growing the circle of your life.

All of these will add up to a beautiful and healthy social community. A value of your circle that will add tremendous value to the whole of your life. Successful and complete people will always have healthy and meaningful social circles in their personal circle.

> We are the average of the five people we spend the most time with.
>
> —Jim Rohn

What a powerful statement this is! When you think about it, this explains the importance of your social circles to the other values of your life. Always make it your priority to eliminate constant drains and virtue thieves from your life's values. In the same way that every other value is interconnected with the others, your social construct will certainly be impactful on the entirety of your life.

> Be careful the environment you choose, for it will shape you; be careful the friends you choose, for you will become like them.
> —W. Clement Stone

7

MIND YOUR TEMPLE

(FITNESS VALUE)

WHAT DO WARREN BUFFET, PRESIDENT OBAMA, Dr. Dre, and Oprah have in common? Besides being household names and having achieved quite respectable notoriety in their fields? They are all avid fans of working out daily and see it as an integral component of their life's success.

There is a myriad of reasons why people that exercise daily do so. For some, it's pure vanity; some do it as a profession, some to thwart generational genetic concerns, some for the camera, and the list goes on. But nearly all successful people not only include a daily exercise regimen in their lives but also see it as integral to their overall success. If the goal is to hang out at the beach all day, you're simply lost. You need clarity of your whole-life purpose so that single values of your circle don't become the entirety of your life.

When we talk about the interconnectedness of the seven values, it becomes easier to see that successful people value fitness not so much as an endgame as the attraction at the beach; rather, they value it as a means to developing mental clarity, toughness, and discipline that will be advantageous to them in their whole lives. The benefits to their overall health are addictive by-products.

One of the greatest commodities a person has is their ability to influence others. Influence... not manipulate or demand! But the ability to persuade others to follow your lead, ideals, strategies, and values. You don't develop the ability to effectively influence by money or position. You do so because people deem you to be believable, having good character and integrity. They follow people who live by convictions and discipline. People who take their lives and their success seriously. People who are following a higher plan for themselves. People will not trustingly follow someone they perceive to be undisciplined. And not taking care of your health and your body is the epitome of an undisciplined mindset.

The benefits of a daily exercise regimen are endless and mirrored by all other areas of life. I'm not talking about doing 20 push-ups twice a week or piddling around with dumbbells in your garage for 10 minutes on Saturday morning. Neither am I suggesting that it must be a hardcore 7-day-a-week 2-hour gym routine. But I am talking about a daily commitment to an exercise program that should at the very least fulfill the following objectives:

- It should challenge you to push yourself.
- It should require some sacrifice and minimal inconvenience.
- It should demand stickability.

- It should involve goals and specific target objectives.

- It should be accompanied by a clean nutritional diet.

- It should include drinking plenty of water.

- It should involve getting proper sleep.

Culture may tip-toe around your unhealthy habits, and politically correct posturing will insulate you from an obvious reality—meaning just because people never address your bad health and conditioning doesn't suggest that everything is fine.

We are in an era when culture teaches you to find creative and innovative arguments to justify your plight rather than figure out how to change. I certainly don't condone shaming people over their weight or size. But if I am your friend and I see you on a course of action or inaction that is detrimental to your longevity, we are going to have a motivating conversation about it. At some point, you must abandon all excuses and simply get healthy.

I realize you may have to undo bad habits that you learned by observation. And you may be eating yourself to an early grave because of severe trauma as a child... the list can go on, and it's real. However, whatever the case is, you need to make the effort to get some help, get into therapy or counseling, and get your head and heart in a better space so you can live. The world is not going to give you complimentary success just because you've had a tough time. You're going to have to work hard at it like everybody else must.

Although I'm not advocating that to be successful you must be ripped to shreds with muscles straining through your clothes. Neither am I trying to shame anyone into being a certain size or weight. Just get healthy. People are attracted to things that are attractive. And the benefits of exercising daily and taking care of your body are very attractive. It may not produce a body that will get you on the cover of *Health and Fitness,* but it will surely produce plenty of other profound benefits such as:

- Confidence in oneself.
- Uncompromising discipline.
- People who take their lives seriously.
- Great energy.
- Noticeable work ethic.

These are just a few.

THE DISCIPLINES NECESSARY TO BE FIT

- Commit to a daily regimen. Preferably same time every day. You can mix up the locations, but the more consistent you can be with a routine, the more likely you are to stick with it.

- Plan your meals before your grocery shopping.

- Plan your exercise. Don't just say you're going to go out and get a little exercise. Plan out your week at the beginning and have what you're going to do each day planned and accounted for.

- Monitor your water intake. Soda doesn't count as your water intake. Neither does wine and beer. Carry a jug around with you and drink throughout the day.

- The discipline to say no to junk. You are what you eat! Avoid the stuff that makes you feel sluggish, gain weight, suffer from heartburn, etc. You can google a million ways to eat healthily.

- Avoiding slumber and inactivity. The experts are now telling us that sitting is the new smoking. Meaning, the adverse effects of sitting around for longer periods of time are doing significant damage to our overall health.

- The acknowledgment of the interconnectedness of fitness to the other values of your life.

THE BENEFITS OF DAILY EXERCISE

- **Clarity of thought.** When you engage in intense physical exercise, your body goes into a "fight or flight" mode which triggers the release of an endorphin called "brain-derived neurotrophic factor (BDNF)" that gives you the ability to think more clearly and better respond to business demands.

- **Exercise nurtures your competitive nature...** even if the opponent is the old version of yourself. Your commitment to being a better version of you will always compete with the old version of you that wants to return to what is comfortable and most familiar. Resist! The disciplines learned and carried out spill over into workplace performance and productivity.

- **Exercise nurtures your problem-solving ability**. Entrepreneurialism is essentially getting paid to problem solve. When you must work through soreness, what exercises work for you and which ones don't, and how to fit them uncompromisingly into your daily schedule, you are developing valuable skills that can only help you and benefit you throughout other areas of your life.

- **Daily exercise assists in your goal-setting skills:** Since exercising naturally produces all kinds of good biological vibes, there's a component of a daily regimen that keeps you reaching for more. As the scale, your clothes, and the mirror become more friendly to you, you will automatically find yourself setting new goals. Adding another mile to your run, or a new specific exercise to your routine. Again, benefits in one value equate to benefits in another.

- **Stickability.** The person who exercises daily has committed to a regimen, dieting, and getting plenty of sleep. So much so that rain, snowy days, and being tired aren't enough to derail your progress. Think of the value of this when it comes to finishing work-related tasks.

Making those necessary sales calls despite a few rejections.

- **Daily exercise gives you an edge.** According to a research study by Vasilios Kosteas, Ph.D., of Cleveland State University, it was established that exercise increases cognitive function and confidence—both building blocks of financial success. Some eye-opening numbers from the study:
  - The income of people who exercise regularly exceeds that of people who mostly sit around by 9%.
  - 5.2% of the time, the income of a person who exercises only one to three times a month exceeds that of someone sedentary.
  - The percentage by which a master's degree raises one's earnings is 6%.
  - A sedentary individual who starts to exercise just a few times per month will see his weekly earnings increase by 2.2%
  - The bottom line was this: The incomes and advancement opportunities are greater for people who exercise regularly. Even more than those with academic degrees.

There are countless other studies that reveal the same truth: People who commit to a daily exercise regimen tend to consistently do better in life and business than those who don't. Therefore, in all your fantasizing about success, you must be proactive and intentional about crafting a daily routine that will have you on your way to being healthy and fit.

8

IMPROVE YOUR FINANCIAL ACUMEN

(FINANCIAL VALUE)

ONE OF THE GREAT TRAGEDIES I RUN ACROSS IN coaching people is that their financial lives are not motivated by good facts, data, and realistic goals. Worse, many of them never connect their money issues to a deficiency in their personal development. Instead, their financial actions and pursuits are more of a reflection of their ego, insecurities, rejection, and a host of other personal deficiencies.

Why did you buy that car you can't afford? Why do you spend money already allocated for something else? What makes you have those "ah forget it" moments when you take a purchase plunge though you're already tapped out?

It's not always because they don't understand basic arithmetic. It has more to do with them not doing the work in other values of their circle.

I wouldn't begin to advise you via a short read here on how to maximize certain investments or what kind of stocks to buy. I am not the guy qualified to do that. I grew up poor without any good examples of financial stewardship and with plenty of examples of how to let scarcity rule your life, decisions, and perspectives. Most of the stability that has come in recent years has been the result of finally getting sick and tired of the plateaus and saying enough is enough.

After surrounding myself with sound financial minds and people who had far better patterns than I ever had in their stewardship of money, I have learned some things that could have easily been put into practice very early on in life. Oh, the power and simplicity of knowing the right things.

In talking to you about increasing your financial acumen. I'm referring to the ability to make good judgments and solid decisions concerning your money that advance your life. Whether it's necessary for your job or not, it's important to increase your personal financial acumen so that it positively supports your total circle rather than distract from it.

UNDERSTANDING THE NATURE OF MONEY

You must avoid the trap of chasing after money and material things as an endgame. Chasing the material nature of money has poor outcomes. Comparison, greed, over-extension, etc. Money can't add value to you as a person. It doesn't make your character better. It doesn't automatically give you happiness or peace. What it does is make it easier for you to experience things, more things than the average. It will take a lot of the stress off you. It will give you more choices. But to maximize the wider range of choices, you need to be sound in your emotions and character.

Money is generally defined as payment for goods and services and repayment of debts in each country or socio-economic context. The main functions of **money** are distinguished as: a medium of exchange; a unit of account; a store of value; and, occasionally, a standard of deferred payment.

> Money is but a token for purposes of exchange.
>
> —Plato

Even the stock market is where people with a lot of money express their confidence in what you'll do with yours. Money is for the purpose of bartering for life sustenance, experiences, and adventures.

How does it become the ultimate pursuit and the standard of measurement of one's self-worth? It is an act of futility to chase after money for the sake of money, then to waste it on things that are expressly for the purpose of impressing others, and then still not have the meaningful experiences and adventures that money should afford you to have.

The fruit of your life should not be enslaved to either the lack of money or the abundance of it. Your life shouldn't dramatically change based on the amount of money you have… perhaps a lot of it can enhance your capacity in life, but you're not relegated to a lack of experience and adventure without it. Money and resources follow vision. The clearer you are on what you're doing and where you're going, money seems to just find you. The healthy yield that money should produce in your life is:

Life Sustenance

The supporting of life or health; the maintenance of essential necessities. In Matthew chapter 6, Jesus spoke extensively about life sustenance—the things you will eat, drink, wear, and where you will live, concluding with the statement, "So do not worry, saying, 'What shall we eat?' or 'What shall we drink?' or 'What shall we wear?' For the pagans run after all these things, and your heavenly Father knows that you need them. But seek first his kingdom and his righteousness, and all these things will be given to you as well."

God knows we have need of basic life sustenance and is more than willing and able to provide those things for us. But your financial goals cannot be confined primarily to this purpose—a bigger house, a nicer car, more clothes, etc. Don't let what should be your basic needs get elevated to your highest of goals. This is all entry-level stuff. Move on to goals that are far more impacting and will outlive you.

Experiences/Adventures

I understand people should save, invest for their retirement, and work for stability and freedom in their golden years. I'm as much a believer in a 401(k), mutual fund investments, and stocks as the next guy. But I am also keenly aware of the fact that people retire on their memories.

Our financial experts tend to embrace hard work and delayed gratification to such an extreme that it's often at the expense of other things that are just as important. There's a real value in earning and saving money. But there's also value in spending money—on the right things. Adventures and memorable experiences with the people most important to you are worthy investments of your money.

There's a certain magic to spending money on adventures and experiences that isn't dissimilar to buying stocks and mutual funds. Invested money—due to compounding interest—doesn't just grow, it grows exponentially. In a very similar way, when you can share wonderful experiences and memories in your older years, those times become in and of themselves, additional experiences. So, just as funds invested in savings and retirement plans yield a rate of return, there's a rate of return on the adventures and experiences you've invested in throughout your life.

Prepping the Next Generation to Bear the Same Fruit

An apple tree bears delicious apples so you can have the pleasure of the fruit, so that you might have a great experience. That experience of eating the apple also involves the seeds within it. You don't have a great experience just so that you can… you nurture the tree to keep producing and you plant the seeds so the next generation can have what you have but in greater abundance. Every generation should be able to stand on the shoulders of the previous one and go further and faster than they did.

Money spent on things that prepare and equip your children or grandchildren to succeed is money wisely spent. Grow the richest life you can; make sure that it is as rich with memories and experiences—rich for all the reasons you accumulated money in the first place. And along the way, you will help your future generations to see the value in meaningful experiences and memories are as important as anything else.

MONEY SIMPLIFIED

I've never been much of a budget guy. I've lived on both ends of the money spectrum. I've had the big house on the hill behind a gate, drove the Rolls Royce, and lived big. I've also had to recover from bad business deals, partners, foolish decisions, etc., and had to fight through the reality of bankruptcy. Any time I've gotten in trouble, it was always because I drifted from one of two things or both.

- **One**: the simplicity of money comprehension
- **Two**: the ultimate endgame money should steer you toward

Let me explain. I asked a very wealthy man who had owned a string of banks in Texas to share his secret with me concerning money and making a lot of it. He and I had just become friends and remain to this day. I was so expecting some deep insight into the mysterious world of the wealthy and then he floored me with simplicity.

His advice was that simple is best. People tend to gravitate to the complex when it comes to money because it makes them feel like they've been let in on some great mystery. The simple truth is that you must have clear vision, not just of what you want financially but also of what you want the totality of your life to look like. What kind of experiences do you desire to have? What kind of lasting adventures do you want to share with the people you care about? Then, you must establish simple patterns and stick to them. "Long-term obedience in the same direction will always get you to a big payday." Your patterns boil down to a strict awareness of three things:

Income

What are your consistent and dependable revenue streams? Don't factor in your bonuses; you'll have them spent before you get them. Don't include extra one-time money; it may only be one time.

Expenses

Fixed expenses and needs. Equal financial attention given to what it takes to live today and what it takes to prepare for your golden years. Needs, not wants.

Reality Check

Periodically, you must weigh expenses against income. If your expenses outweigh your income, you must dial it down. Sell some stuff; simplify your life rather than bust your butt trying to increase your income overnight. You won't be in the proper headspace when you're trying to earn to keep up. There's a difference between being content and being satisfied. It's not going to take away from your earning mojo to be happy with what you have. Contentment will put you in a better frame of mind to be more creative, innovative, and tenacious.

Is it imperative that you live in the 10,000-square-foot house, or will a 2,000 one do for now? Do you have to have three cars or will one or two do for a while? Do you have what you have because you need it for personal contentment, or are you trying to keep up with people who aren't impressed anyway and probably don't even notice?

Then he shared this with me. There are three types of mindsets people have.

Consumers

Life is happening for me. This is where most people live. It represents the masses. Get everything you can get now, use it up, and then get some more. If they see it, they want it, and they'll run themselves ragged to get it. Consumers tend to spend more time chasing after vanities.

"Vanities" is an old English word originating with soap makers. When all the mixed ingredients would come to a boil these incredible-looking bubbles would begin to float upwards. They looked so substantive… like you could grab them and frame them or put them on display somewhere. But as soon as they'd touch one, it would burst, and they would be left with sticky soap suds in their hands. They called these bubbles vanities.

Consumers are slaves to soap bubbles. They are motivated by these fantastical ideas that certain material things are going to change their life. They *must* have them. Then when they get them, at almost any cost, they aren't what they thought they were. There's nothing left but sticky soap suds in their hands.

While there may be a little bit of consumer in all of us, it's being a typical consumer-minded person that you want to grow past. This mindset can make you more susceptible to manipulation. Consumers can be swayed to get the newest and most updated gadgets. From phones and services to fads and trends. Vendors can always count on consumers to do whatever they have to do to get the latest thing. Consumer psychologists refer to it as "behaviorism." Meaning you are driven by external stimuli and can almost always be convinced to do things because of some outside influence.

Most of us chuckle at the example of a teenager who must have the absolute newest iPhone. They'll be laughed at for having "that iPhone that is sooo six months ago." Their self-worth, their popularity, and perhaps even their destiny is connected to their need for it. The consumer parent will argue dismissively about how silly that is, all the while they are the same. It's just bigger toys, older friends, and less time, so more urgency to everything.

Stewards

Life is happening to me. Protect, guard, and scarcity is their prevalent mindset. They're always careful... too careful. They won't take their family on vacation or go camping together because it might take away from their savings. They have everything looking solid and substantial on paper, but the people they care about grow up without adventure and with few noteworthy experiences to enrich their lives. They don't know how to live a little bit. They agonize over budgets, retirement plans, IRAs, etc. They are always concerned with how many slices they can get out of the pie rather than seeing that there are plenty of pies.

Producers

Life is responding to me. This is the mindset that sees money correctly and positively. Producers tend to take more responsibility for what they have and why they have it. They don't appreciate being manipulated into things, nor are they content to shrivel into a cocoon of scarcity. They understand that life will respond to them and their actions and choices. If they make wise choices, life will yield positively for them. They are always looking to solve problems, produce things, and innovate experiences and adventures to make the lives of the people around them better.

Most often, it is people that think like producers that are much better at being congruent with the income/expense/reality check equation. Further, it is the producer category in which you are far more likely to witness the makings of sustainable wealth.

9

YOUR QUALITY-OF-LIFE IQ

TO CREATE SOME SPACE FOR YOU TO EFFECtively address your success matrix, you need to employ a filtering system: an automated way of measuring all your thoughts, actions, pursuits, and activities. The seven-valued life matrix in and of itself gives you a big head start in this already. But I'm referring to an additional internal awareness that allows you to accurately and expediently discern the things that are positively contributing to the growth of your success matrix versus the things that are adversarial to it.

It's surprising how many people will construct a dream board, set some goals, or embrace a new determination to change their life without addressing the primary components of influence. They remain unaware of the people, language, activities, and habits/patterns that are hindering their progress.

Specifically, do you know if the people you spend the most time with are helping you move closer to having it all, or are they pulling you away from it? Often, the people closest to you will unconsciously pull on you negatively. The short answer to this is that mediocrity always attacks excellence. Your forward progress can put them on the spot and make them feel uncomfortable if they're not committed to the same pursuit that you are.

> You will be the same person in five years as you are today except for the people you meet and the books you read.
> –Charlie "Tremendous" Jones

I was working with a particular athlete several years ago who had won a championship title in his sport that translated into millions of dollars. He wouldn't own up to his strange loyalty to his "homeboys" and how negatively it was affecting his ability to sustain his success. While he was moving into his destiny, his entourage was inadvertently dragging him back to the man they were familiar and most comfortable with. The hard truth is this… not everybody who has accompanied your initial phase of progress will be able to continue with you.

The sad conclusion is that this gentleman ended up losing his millions and is now trying to figure out how to rebuild and regain what he once had. He's discovering that it's a lot harder the second time around.

Developing a higher "quality of life IQ" may prove to be easier than you thought. Discerning the nature and influence of places, people, and patterns is easy enough. It's the unwavering commitment and diligence in follow-through that takes more time.

> Victory at all costs, victory despite all terror, victory however long and hard the road may be; for without victory, there is no survival.
> —Winston Churchill

CHANGE YOUR WORLD/METRON

A little bit of reverse engineering here… Change your world by changing your patterns. Change your patterns by changing your actions. Change your actions by changing your thoughts. Change your thoughts by changing your vocabulary. We could probably get technical here and continue this progression for a good while. There is a process to a personal culture shift. At each level, you must sustain the disruption to initiate change at the next level. Here's one idea of progression:

- Words create thoughts.
- Sustained thoughts result in images.
- Images produce action/movement.
- Sustained action/movement turn into patterns.
- Sustained patterns become your rhythm.
- Sustained rhythm produces your destiny.

"Sustain" is the operative word in this chapter. I live here in Houston, Texas. We are known for having two seasons: warm and hot, with a year-round humidity average of over 90%. In the years I've lived here, it has snowed maybe three times. It even stayed on the ground for a few days. However, you would be hard-pressed to find a store anywhere around here to buy skis, snowmobiles, or a good variety of sub-zero outdoor clothing. No need.

You don't build on something that rare that may not happen again for a few years. On the other hand, I have great friends in North Pole, Alaska. You'll find a plethora of that stuff there and all year around.

Atmosphere is defined as the primary tone or mood of a place *at the moment*. Atmospheres experience disruptions all the time, but the only way you establish a new climate is if those disruptions are sustained.

Climate is defined as the pervading conditions of a region — be it the weather or an aspect of life — that over a prolonged period establish normal. Culture grows out of prolonged normal.

Therefore, people often find themselves being inspired by being around someone successful or accomplished in some way. They decide to change — they want more for themselves. However, a year later, very little has changed. Why?

Perhaps because after having a moment of inspiration, they returned to the environment they were accustomed to. The same boring people, with boring ideas (if any ideas at all), the same boring excuses, and all the same limitations.

They didn't bother to identify the characteristics of the atmosphere they were inspired and challenged in, so they were unaware of what they needed to do to sustain it. They thought they could return to their same atmosphere of mediocrity with a few new ideas and success would find them.

In the process of addressing your circle for success, it will be imperative that you carefully examine some things. You will have to look at the people, the activities, the events, and the experiences that take up most of your time, focus, and attention. Then determine whether they are moving you forward constructively or holding you back destructively.

You would never take a thousand dollars and put it into an account or a stock that had no ROI (return on investment). You're not going to be willing to put your money into something that's going to eat up your money or sit there for 20 years with no growth. You carefully examine the investment. How has it performed in the past? What are the indicators that it will do well now? Once you have a reasonable level of confidence that it is a worthwhile investment, then you pull the trigger. My point here is that you need to have a process, a system, your own personal barometer to help you determine if what you are going to put your time, money, energy, and focus into is worthwhile.

This applies to activities, habits, relationships, etc. Not everybody should get your attention. Everything doesn't necessarily deserve the full weight of your support. You only have so much time, energy, and personal resources to go around. You must measure everything and manage yourself well.

To summarize here, you can't just do something good or special over a weekend and think the entire climate of your circle is going to permanently shift. You must take responsibility for the climate of your life as well. A shift in your "personal atmosphere" is necessary and a great start. But if you want that atmosphere to become your new "normal," you must manage yourself and your circle. And the great news is that if you'll stay at it, you'll eventually change your climate.

10

SYSTEMS FOR CIRCLE BUILDING

IF YOU'RE THINKING YOU WOULD NEED TO BE darn near superhuman to accomplish total completeness, you may still be looking at this task from a one-at-a-time perspective. The challenge usually centers around our erroneous idea of what perfection is. To the average westerner, it implies being flawless or needing no improvement. In chapter one, I referred to the ancient Greek word *teleios* to define perfection more accurately. It means "development or completion of growth in all of its parts."

Every faith practice on the planet subscribes to this idea of perfection, achieved one way or through one process or another. However, few are suggesting "flawless."

In looking at the seven-value "metron" I have provided, a better idea begins to emerge. It suggests that the way to create sustainable momentum is to develop each of your values with equal amounts of attention, energy, and effort. Simply...

> The way to address the matrix of success is to ascribe to each of the seven parts the same value, therefore applying the same attention, effort, diligence, and reverence to each value.

One could look at this and think, "Wow, that's a lot to tend to. I don't know how I would keep track of all of that." But, if you could develop a system that allowed you to equally develop each value simultaneously, then it comes into a hopeful perspective, especially if your systematic approach is, in large part, automated.

This doesn't mean that you must be always hitting a grand slam in every value. It simply means that there's growth and forward progress always happening.

SUCCESS IS A SYSTEM

Whether you personally like McDonald's or not, you must agree that they are a hugely successful organization. The reason why their French Fries are highly likely to taste the same in the USA, Europe, Africa, or Rio De Janeiro is because of their systematic processes.

Regardless of who's working, how old they are, or whether they're in a good mood or bad one, there is a systematic process that regulates how everything is prepared. Everything is always prepared the same way, cooked at the same temperature, for the same length of time, etc. They have an automated system that ensures the consistency of their product. The outcome of their product is not relegated by any individual employee. It is the system that produces the product.

Similarly, whether you are trying to build a church, a baseball team, a corporation, a family, a community, or your own personal physique, the set of principles you must follow are the same. The methodology of implementation may vary, but the principles at their core are the same.

The principles necessary to build a great business are the same ones required to build a great family. You build a great physique the same way you build a great community. Your financial portfolio is developed in the same way your social circle is built. And so on.

Success is not a mystery or hidden secret reserved for the elite of the world. It's not a particular gene or biological advantage. It's not a one-time random achievement.

Success is a set of values, perspectives, and disciplines that, when followed systematically, yield a specific outcome. Followed consistently, they produce consistent outcomes.

Most people have managed to experience at least a small measure of success in one area of their life, from doing well for a particular semester of school to following a certain recipe to make a masterful dessert or a myriad of possibilities in between. Perhaps it's the way you've approached building a family or growing your business. Or the disciplined and systematic approach to developing a great physique. In any event, it is highly unlikely that someone has gone through life and never succeeded at *anything*.

The reason that many people do not move consistently toward an abundant and complete life, is this: They failed to ascribe equal importance and priority to the full range of values in their life, therefore, not committing the same level of focused attention, diligence, and perseverance to their entire circle. Then, even when they have done well in one value, the failure in another adds a bitter taste to the victory they have achieved.

> The time, effort, and attention you give to a thing will always mirror the value you have put on it.

You must be able to see the cause-and-effect dynamic and the interconnectedness of all seven values. If not, you get stuck looking at one value at a time, and usually the one that is in a crisis. You must be able to see and appreciate the various realities:

- A great home/family life can energize you to be creative and innovative in building a business and making money.
- When you exercise and get healthy, your mind, stamina, and self-image are better. You want to get out and do more.
- Financial opportunities seem to find people that others believed to be disciplined.

- Good emotional intelligence will make you a social circle genius.
- The pursuit of God causes a redemptive quality to touch everything in your life and make it better.

I could fill pages with examples of the interconnectedness of your values, but I think you get the point.

This one-value concept of success must come to an end for you. You *can* have it all. If you've ever succeeded at *anything* in your life, then you can succeed in every area that really matters.

SUCCESS LEAVES CLUES

The reason I am confident that you can be amazingly successful is because every person that has ever "had it all" has left us a blueprint, a collection of clues as to how they achieved it. And when studied carefully, it is apparent that there is nothing to it that the ordinary man/woman can't do. There are common denominators that weave through the path and processes of all of them. In classic Hansel and Gretel fashion, they have all left a trail of clues that will lead any who are courageous enough to follow, to the life of their dreams.

When you mimic the mindset, patterns, and disciplines of the successful, you wake up one day and realize that you have become one of them.

SUCCESS IS TRANSFERRABLE

As I've already stated, let me say again... the set of principles, perspectives, patterns, and disciplines that produce a measure of success in one area, can absolutely be applied to other life values and yield the same kind of success. What built a great marriage will build a great business. What renders a great family will build a great church. What builds a healthy body and fitness lifestyle, will also contribute to a great community. The disciplines in creating a healthy financial portfolio will also yield a healthy physique. The challenge will always center around your values. There will always be enough time to address the things that matter to you. It may not be your lack of knowledge as to how to advance areas of your life as much as it is whether these areas are of the same value to you. These seven life values are not unlike each other. They have been wired to respond similarly to the same kind of stimuli.

The real question that most people subconsciously wonder about is this: *"How do I make something matter to me that has never really mattered before?"*

That's a very credible question. If certain life values weren't important enough to the generation before you to model them effectively, then it's not likely that they will be very high on your priority list either.

Each of the seven life values is interconnected and interactive with each other. The dismissal or minimization of one has a significantly negative effect on the others. This must be realized and always taken into consideration.

If you grew up in an overweight household where eating habits, attitudes toward exercise, and basic life patterns were reflective of that reality, you are more likely to have a dismissive perspective toward being fit. You'd rather focus on close family relationships. And close family relationships are very important. However, if you can see that your ability to do certain activities with your family is affected by a lack of fitness, perhaps you'd put more value on the importance of health. If you could realize that your life span, earning window, and quality of life could be adversely affected by you dying way too early (especially if you could have done something about it), perhaps you'd put more value on your health. Similar scenarios can be said about the interactive relationship between all the seven values.

When you realize this and learn to respect it as a reality, you are well on your way to completeness. The healthy and productive perspective of managing your entire circle with equal amounts of focus, effort, and energy in a systematic and thorough way is the next piece of the puzzle.

BUILD A SYSTEM, AND IT WILL BUILD YOU A LIFE.

A system is defined as a set of principles or procedures by which something is done, an organized scheme or method; this is a system. If you do a particular thing every day, it's a system.

Developing systems will help you gain back lost time. It will help you eliminate procrastination. Systems help you reduce the chaos in your life into manageable tasks. Systematic living helps you constantly do the things that are important instead of waiting to address them when they've become critically urgent. Systems help you harness the power of a habit or a pattern. When you develop the habit of doing things in a systematic way, you will dramatically increase your effectiveness and aid in your own self-mastery.

> It's not what we do occasionally that shapes our lives. It's what we do consistently.
> –Anthony Robbins

You can be systematic about nearly everything. More specifically, however, let's talk about building a system of activity, time investment, and vital attention that addresses and improves your seven life values. It is incredibly beneficial to get focused on the things that coincide with your values.

Often when working with executives or professionals, once I convince them to stop lying to themselves and everyone around them, I will ask them to show me their schedules. On their Google calendars, you will see everything from conference calls, staff meetings, product roll-out dates, business trips, doctor's appointments, etc. When I ask them to show me where they've scheduled a date with their spouse or quality time with their children, they look at me like a deer in headlights or mutter some lame excuse like, "Those things are supposed to be spontaneous." As opposed to not happening at all? This excuse is usually code for "it isn't happening at all."

> If it matters, schedule it. If it gets scheduled, it gets done. If not, it usually doesn't even get remembered.

The rules are: If it matters, schedule it. If it gets scheduled, it gets done. If it doesn't get scheduled, it usually doesn't even get remembered. This is especially important in the beginning of your renewed pursuit of completeness. Until you become established and habitual about the patterns in your life, you must be more than diligent about scheduling.

When you live your life propelled by an intentional system, it will make you look like a time management genius! Eliminating activities that waste irreplaceable time and replacing them with specific actions that effectively address your circle, will render time you never knew you had.

> Success is the sum of small efforts repeated day in and day out.
>
> –Robert Collier

The average American spends 11 hours per day watching videos, browsing social media, posting/interacting on Facebook, and doing other similar tasks on their smartphones. I'm aware that some of our lives have become totally interlinked with our smart devices, and some of that time is productive—but eleven hours?

Times are changing rapidly, technology advances quickly, and our way of doing life has to adjust to these. But, before these new demands sneak up on us, you need to have a system in place that will continue to help you self-regulate the investment of your time, energy, and focus.

> There is never enough time to do everything, but there is always enough time to do the most important things. What are they?
>
> —Brian Tracy

Building personal systems takes some work and commitment, but it's not as exhausting as one would think. Perhaps this will help.

ASSESS YOUR STEWARDSHIP

None of us are unlimited when it comes to our personal life resources. We all have a measured amount of energy, time, and focus capacity to work with. A successful person will always be cognizant of how they are stewarding their personal resources. Consequently, you must be able to identify the worthiness of anything or anybody that requests the investment of your time, energy, and focus.

Not everybody has to have you. Not everyone deserves you. Not everyone to whom you are giving unfettered access to your life knows how to appreciate it or even what to do with it. Some things that you are so sure will fall apart without your intense focus, may surprise you and continue to blossom just fine. Not every activity is going to move your life forward.

Hopefully these are some of the realizations you will come to when you really start assessing how you steward yourself.

There's an adage that says, "Never stay too long where you are tolerated; go instead to where you are celebrated."

I'm sure extreme applications of this can be argued against, but nonetheless, it's an adage that gives way to many variations that are very powerful and thought-provoking. Truths and principles that must be considered when you are evaluating your personal stewardship.

For example, "Don't stay positioned in a place where you are giving out disproportionately more than you are receiving." We are not wired to function indefinitely in a state of deficit. You may be able to compensate for a season of time, but when there's a deficit in your life that lasts too long, there will eventually be a collapse or an implosion.

So, as a foundational aspect of self-stewardship assessment, there are four things you will need to do well, which includes doing them with honesty and transparency:

1. You must be aware of the people and activities that pull energy and virtue out of you without putting anything back into you. You must effectively manage to whom or to what you give your time and energy.

2. Guard your life ferociously against those things trying to return to your life or you returning to them.

3. Find, develop, or invent new activities, relationships, and adventures that put at least an equal amount of benefit back into you as what they pull out of you. Focus on the things that replenish you with energy and virtue.

4. You must discipline yourself to stay committed to those new patterns, activities, and relationships.

Effective assessment begins with explicit clarity concerning your desired outcome and your commitment to it. It will lead to unprecedented and unparalleled momentum in your circle that leads to fulfillment and joy that remains a rarity to most people. Not just a goal or target in one single value, but a dream that you can "have it all!"

Therefore, it is the equal and simultaneous development of all seven life values that must be your objective in evaluating your self-stewardship. You start by assessing as much of your life and activity as possible. Make a list of everything you do on a regular basis.

- Meal prepping and grocery shopping
- When you pay your bills
- How much time you spend talking to friends and acquaintances and how much of that time is productive
- When you exercise
- Working around the house/yard
- When you answer emails and peruse through your social media
- Returning phone calls and doing reports.
- Family activities and leisure time

- Personal hobbies
- Self-improvement time: reading, prayer/meditation

Everyone's list will look a bit different. Productive assessment involves being able to identify where your time, energy, and attention regularly go. When your list is complete you need to ask yourself these questions:

- What are the things that drain you the most?
- What frustrates you?
- What is adding value to your life?
- Where are you wasting a lot of time?
- What are you doing that is counterproductive?
- Where can you be more efficient?
- Where are you losing time and/or money?
- What is missing? (Date nights, quality time spent with your kids, collective family activities)

There may be things sapping the life out of you that don't need to be eliminated; they simply need to be renovated. For example, it's possible that while evaluating, you determine that most of the recent dates with your spouse have not been light and refreshing, due to too much tension and draining arguments. Obviously, you don't need to stop that or eliminate it from your life, but perhaps you need some new ground rules:

- No talking about money issues on dates.
- No talking about current challenges.
- No griping allowed.
- No "I just have to get this off my chest."

I was talking to a friend of mine, trying to help him, and his response to this was, "Good Lord, what's left to do?" You could always determine that on dates, you're only allowed to reminisce about times that made you laugh. You must stick with talking about memories that warm your heart. Talk about the events in the past that had such a positive impact on your life. Perhaps you can focus on creating some new ones. I think you get the point.

Once you've either highlighted or eliminated things from your list, you now know what to start scheduling. The things you have separated from the list and identified as being productive, constructive, and replenishing are what you start with. Begin to arrange these things in a systematic way that can be scheduled as regular occurrences and activities.

PLAN YOUR PATTERNS

When you commit to living your life through a system, you will greatly reduce the disruptions in your life and prevent them from turning into rabbit trails of urgency. When you've sufficiently answered the previous questions, you can then begin to develop patterns that keep you aimed toward equally developing your seven life values. A great way to start is by arranging your daily activities in a way that addresses all your circle in small daily increments.

SYSTEMS FOR CIRCLE BUILDING

There is a quite effective format or template for developing a weekly routine that will catapult your life forward. Make sure that your life schedule has allowed for and is conducive to the following (each of these in every 24-hour period):

- A daily time to reflect in solitude. Meditation and prayer. A time for your own personal devotion.

- Time spent on personal growth. Reading relevant material that further empowers you to be more proficient at leading in the seven life values. I would suggest that you not try to indulge in large quantities all at once. I personally am always reading at least three to four books simultaneously. But I read one or two chapters daily in each.

- Reflective exercises through which you practice breathing, controlling physiology, and contemplating how to strategically respond to scenarios that normally challenge you emotionally.

- A time to engage in a meaningful way with your spouse each day. It doesn't require a date every night, just once a week. But you should plan for daily time to converse, share, reflect, and dream together.

- Quality time with your children. Children spell love t-i-m-e. Develop a pattern of daily communication and involvement. School activities, homework, sports practice, or simply family games occasionally. You're not too busy. If you are, then you're too busy to succeed. You will always have time for the things that matter. The average lion spends 20 hours a day resting/sleeping. Yet, it manages to do enough in two to three hours a day to maintain its reputation as king of the safari. Think on that for a minute!

- A time to reach out to include your friends.
- Your commitments to daily exercise. It doesn't require a gym membership. Just start moving more. Park your car further away from entrances. Take brisk walks around the block every time you leave the house as well as when you return—this can do wonders for you. Clean up your eating habits. Drink plenty of water. Get enough sleep. Every little bit helps.
- A time to budget, assess, and plan for your financial future. You need to give daily attention—not obsession—just energy spent on evaluating whether you're on target to reach incremental financial goals. These are great times to reflect on your personal financial stewardship—are you spending money on unnecessary things, or obsessing over toys and material things?

Again, I can't stress enough that these are tasks/habits that must be scheduled and practiced daily!

EXECUTE YOUR PLAN

Inaction is the enemy of success. The most difficult step in any process typically is execution. Planning, dreaming, strategizing—far easier to do than execution. Unsuccessful people take forever to decide, and when they finally do, they're most likely to change their minds more than once. Successful people learn how to pull the trigger quickly, take swift massive action, and almost never change their minds about it.

If you want this pursuit of completeness to work, then you must get ferocious about executing your plan. Remind yourself that all the strategizing and planning in the world becomes an act of futility without execution.

Don't try to initiate too many things all at once. Steve Jobs of Apple would take his top 100 people on a retreat every year. They would brainstorm and write hundreds of potential ideas on a large whiteboard. Then Jobs would ask: "What are the ten things we should be doing next?" After significant discussion, the group would come up with a list of ten. Then Jobs would slash the bottom seven and announce, "We can only do three."

Execution isn't about finality or crossing the finish line in world record time. It's about getting started on patterns that will eventually become automated. Patterns that will move your circle toward perfection/completion.

Set alarms for certain tasks and times, ask people close to you to hold you accountable, and do whatever you have to do to stick with your plan. "Success is life's reward when you stop making excuses."

> Plenty of proper preparation prevents the possibility of a poor performance.
> —Unknown

IMPROVE YOUR SYSTEM

You need to re-assess from time to time whether some of your patterns are working for you. The quickest way to fall away from systematic living is to continue doing certain things for too long that are not producing. The system is not an end. You're not awesome because you live systematically. You become awesome when your personal system is producing a complete circle. You wouldn't indefinitely tolerate an employee who wasn't producing or, worse yet, was working against you. You need to fire some of your patterns occasionally.

Tony Robbins said, "Businesses don't fail because of the people they hire. They fail more so because of the people they refuse to fire."

So true in your personal life. We all have had bad patterns, destructive habits, or time wasters at some point. No shame in that. It's when you can recognize something wasteful, inefficient, or destructive and you don't replace it… that's when you have some serious problems.

Take the process of self-evaluation seriously. It's your life, your future, and your destiny we're talking about. Never let it be said that you were someone with loads of potential but never realized it. Never let people, toxic relationships, bad patterns and habits, and destructive perspectives be the cause of you not reaching your fullest potential.

YOU ARE THE CEO OF YOUR OWN LIFE.

You can have it all! You *can* develop and live a complete life that yields great fulfillment and satisfaction. But you must accept the fact that you are the CEO of your own life. You must manage the systems that run your life. Your personal atmosphere and climate, your personal culture, and all the contributors to it are your responsibility.

The great news is that you won't have to do it alone. When Jesus said in Matthew 5:48, "Be perfect, therefore, as your heavenly Father is perfect," He meant it. He has a completely reasonable expectation that you be perfect and complete. That also means that if Jesus has that expectation of us, He will certainly equip and empower us as well.

He will help you in every way necessary to live the Complete Life. He has committed to provide for you:

DISCERNMENT

> *But solid food is for the mature, for those who have their powers of discernment trained by constant practice to distinguish good from evil.*
>
> —Hebrews 5:14

God will help you with the ability to determine not only the difference between good and evil but also between what is good and beneficial to you and your quest to live the complete life. Not just "is it good or is it bad," but "is it good for me and my house?"

If you ask, He will also empower you to develop consistency. The key phrase in the verse above is "constant practice."

A STRATEGY

> *Beloved, I wish above all things that thou mayest prosper and be in health, even as thy soul prospers.*
>
> —3 John 1:2

If you think that God's only concern when it comes to your life is where you'll spend eternity, then you're mistaken. His gospel is a holistic gospel. God wants His presence, wisdom, and grace to touch every area of your life. Your whole circle!

WISDOM

> *If any of you lacks wisdom, let him ask God, who gives generously to all without reproach, and it will be given him.*
>
> —James 1:5

It has often been defined that knowledge is the accumulation of ideas, information, and data. Wisdom is the administration of knowledge. Wisdom is what will help you know what to do with what you know. This is important because once you learn a few things, have some principles taught to you, or discover them yourself, and you get exposed to strategies that have proven to work for so many others, you need to know how to apply and execute them in your own life. God promises to give you wisdom simply because you asked for it.

> My son, if you receive my words and treasure up my commandments with you, making your ear attentive to wisdom and inclining your heart to understanding; yes, if you call out for insight and raise your voice for understanding, if you seek it like silver and search for it as for hidden treasures, then you will understand the fear of the Lord and find the knowledge of God. (Prov. 2:1–5)

STRENGTH

> *Do not grieve, for the joy of the Lord is your strength.*
>
> —Nehemiah 8:10

There will be times in the process of pursuing the complete life that you will feel totally spent and that you don't have what it takes to see things through. Those are the times you lean into God and the strength He provides. He promises it, and He will give it.

Psalm 46:1–3 says, "God is our refuge and strength, an ever-present help in trouble. Therefore, we will not fear, though the earth gives way and the mountains fall into the heart of the sea, though its waters roar and foam and the mountains quake with their surging."

Ever-present means exactly that—His strength is *always* there for you. Simply declare what Exodus 15:2 says: "The LORD is my strength and my defense; he has become my salvation. He is my God, and I will praise him, my father's God, and I will exalt him."

11

STELLAR WORK ETHIC

AS THE CEO OF YOUR OWN LIFE AND FUTURE, a stellar work ethic is absolutely required. As I have previously stated, the principles of success are consistent, duplicatable, and transferrable. Consider a strong work ethic to be one of those principles. These are the defining qualities that must show up in all your efforts and in all your values. Some of these I have already covered, but let me put them in principle form:

ALWAYS SHOW UP.

Your family, your future, and your entire circle can never experience a part-time you. Wherever you are, be there! *Don't burden the present with the weight of the past or future.*

You must always show up as a parent. You need to always show up as a spouse. Stay dedicated to every single one of your daily tasks as if you were getting paid and evaluated for it.

Always showing up doesn't just mean being there and expecting everyone to appreciate that you tried. Showing up means being willing to put in the hard work, and then being willing to stay and put in some overtime. Keep showing up—wash, rinse, and repeat. When it's working, *keep doing it!* Employ the seven Ps of success modality:

> Plenty of Proper Preparation Prevents the Possibility of a Poor Performance.

CREATE WHEN AND WHERE NECESSARY BUT LEARN FROM THOSE AHEAD OF YOU.

Copy the patterns of the super successful. Rise up early, read a lot, schedule your life, carefully choose your friends, work hard, clearly define what matters most to you, and learn to say no.

BE INTENTIONAL IN YOUR PLANNING.

The plans may not always work out but *planning always works out*. If you don't have a plan to succeed, you're planning to fail (Proverbs 21:5). Schedule everything that matters. If it doesn't get scheduled, it doesn't get done. Schedule your day the night before: devotions, work, family time, dating your spouse, exercise, reading/personal improvement, and social activity. Stick to the schedule as much as possible but be flexible—stay focused on the objective.

REFLECT OFTEN AND REFLECT PRODUCTIVELY.

At the end of your week, reflect on the things you have done. What worked? Then seek to improve for the week to come. Act like your time and energy is something that must be budgeted just like money.

BE DEPENDABLE.

If you say you're going to do something…, *do it*!

Learn to be positively discriminate—say no when you need to and yes when you should, but don't leave anything in the land of vague ambiguity.

SET A STANDARD OF EXCELLENCE.

Set your own standard of high-quality output, then do everything according to the standard.

> Perfection is not attainable, but if we chase perfection, we can catch excellence.
>
> –Vince Lombardi

Someone once said, "Excellence is not always about doing big grandiose exploits, but it is about doing the small simple things in a big grandiose way." That's how excellence becomes your norm. It defines your mindset and the attitude you approach all of life with.

> Ideas are yesterday, execution is today, and excellence will see you into tomorrow.
>
> —Julian Hall

BE AUDACIOUS.

Don't let mistakes ruin your forward progress. Great CEOs have an ability that is often mistaken as narcissism. I disagree much of the time. I call it audacious resilience. You must have the ability to immediately bounce back from failure.

Lastly, I want to assure you that I am here to cheer you on as well. Our company, Circlebuilders.org, puts on "Circle Builders" collectives and intensives designed to come alongside you with everything we possibly can to help you grow your circle.

We have produced an app that is designed to help you get your life and patterns automated. *It's called the "Circle Builders" app, available on either Apple or Google Play.* Download it and get started immediately. The app will assist you with the following:

- A storehouse of resources and tools for you.
- A staff of quality mentors, people who are experts in their respective fields/values, that are active and accessible.
- A community of like-minded people who are themselves growing the complete circle and

STELLAR WORK ETHIC

living life abundantly, that are free to interact and share their experiences.

- Weekly tasks/assignments to help you jumpstart your circle management.
- There's even a way to assess month to month how your circle is taking shape.
- Podcasts, filmed discussions, and constant updates on our activities and events.

All of this is on the Circle Builders app. It is our gift to you.

So, there you have it: The premise, the information, the challenge, and the tools to be successful at it. Now it's up to you to pull the trigger. Time for you to knock it out of the park. As your life becomes the perfect or complete life, you'll be forever grateful that you did. So will your future generations. You got this!

Lastly, I invite you to visit our website if you haven't already and join our community of circle builders: CircleBuilders.org

www.ingramcontent.com/pod-product-compliance
Lightning Source LLC
Chambersburg PA
CBHW022113090426
42743CB00008B/836